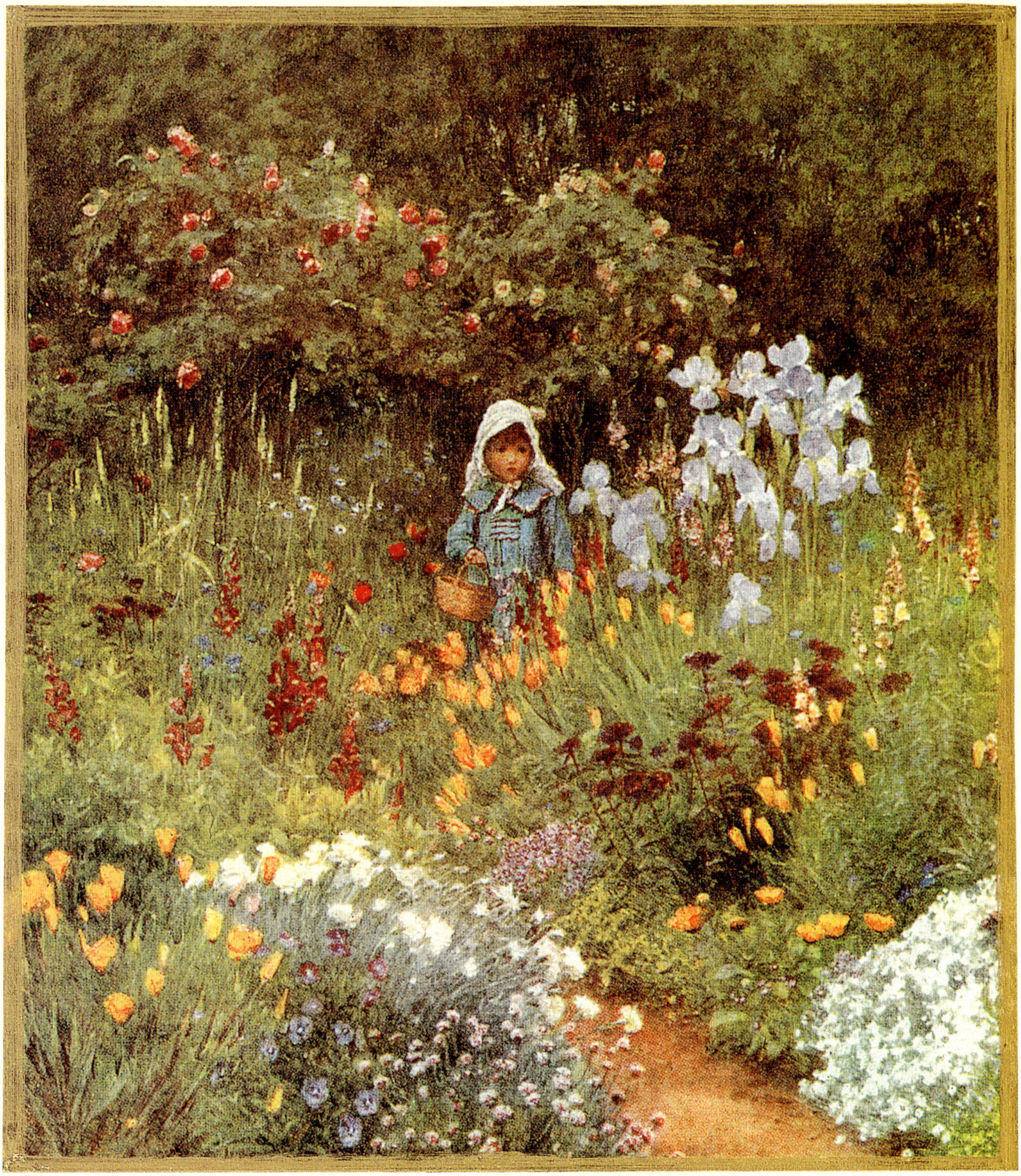

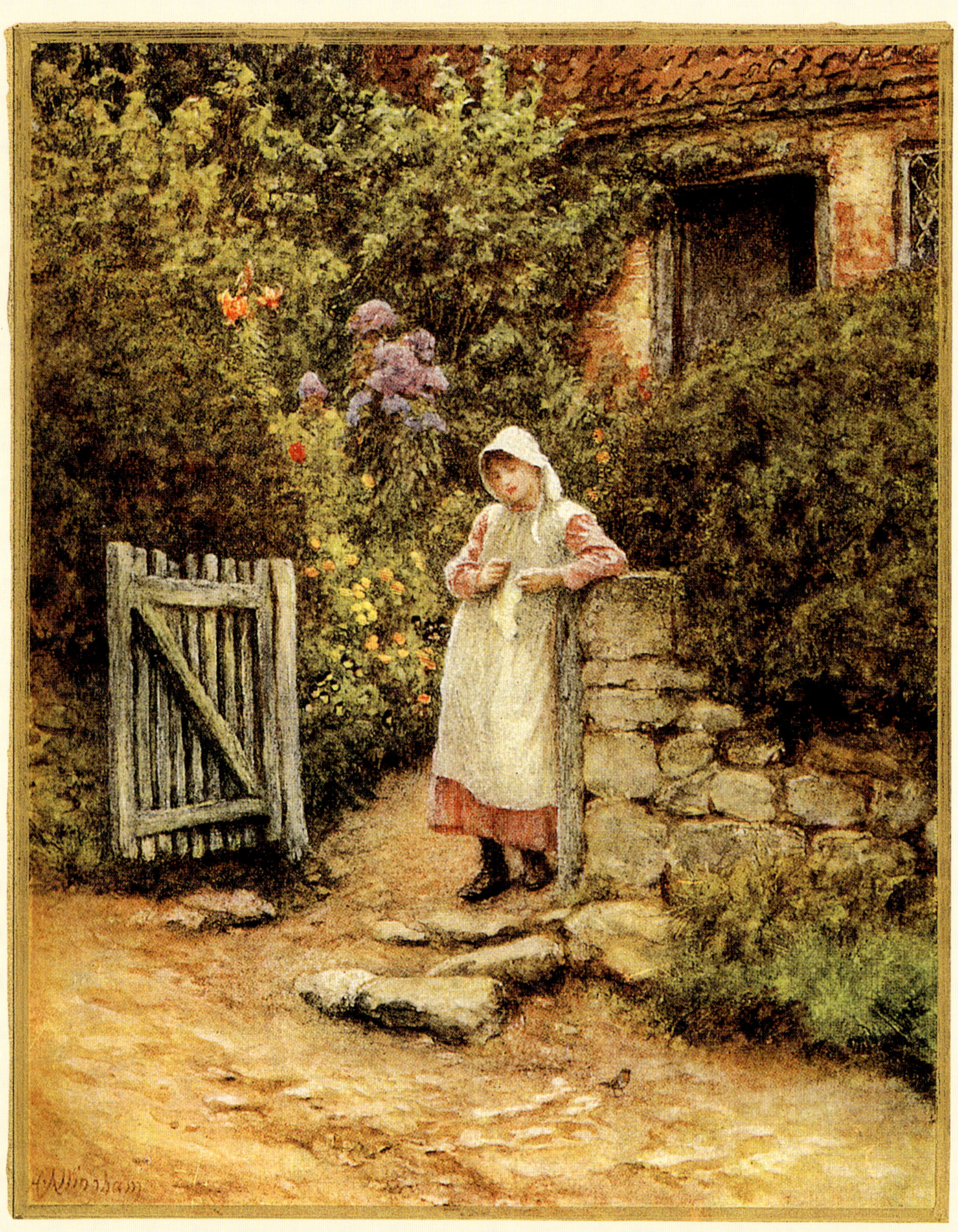
H. Allingham

The Victorian World of
Helen Allingham

Edited by J. Marsden
The Paintings of Helen Allingham

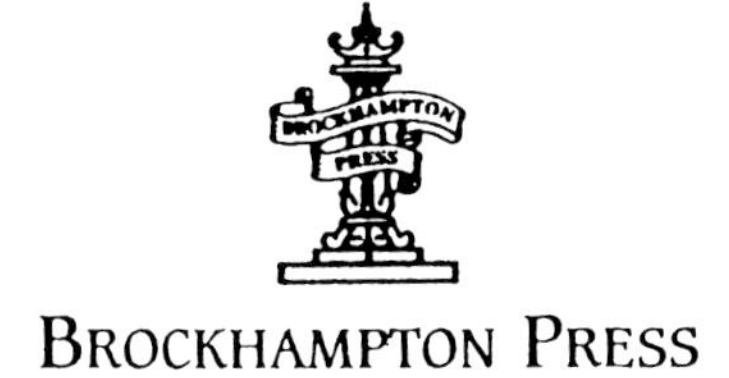

BROCKHAMPTON PRESS

The Victorian World of
Helen Allingham

First published by Brockhampton Press Ltd
20 Bloomsbury Street
London WC1B 3QA

© Brockhampton Press Ltd, 1999

ISBN 1 86019 949 6

Conceived and designed by Savitri Books Ltd

Printed and bound by
APP Printing, Singapore

CONTENTS

INTRODUCTION

Helen Allingham painted a portrait of an England that is long gone. Indeed, it was fast disappearing even as she worked – the cottages that made her famous were being demolished or refurbished in the name of progress as early as the 1880s. She has left us an accurate – if rose-tinted – record of what she saw. Her attention to architectural detail is remarkable, and her concern to portray flowers as more than an amorphous blob of colour led her to develop innovative techniques involving blades, hard brushes, pointed sticks and any other device that suited her purpose.

The text of this book is drawn largely from a memoir by Marcus B. Huish, published in 1903. Huish was a distinguished painter in his own right and at one time Director of the Fine Arts Society. He knew Helen Allingham well and was in a unique position to appreciate both her natural talent and her technical prowess. He also pays generous tribute to her achievement as a woman competing triumphantly in what was very much a man's world.

THE YOUNG CUSTOMERS
painted 1875

Helen Allingham made her name with this watercolour, based on an earlier black and white drawing made as an illustration to a then popular story: A Flat Iron for a Farthing. The watercolour earned her admission into the Society of Painters in Water Colours in 1875. Ruskin saw it and in the notes he always compiled on the Summer Exhibitions he wrote: "The drawing... is for ever lovely – a thing which I believe Gainsborough would have given one of his own paintings for, old fashioned as red-tipped daisies are, and more precious than rubies". The watercolour was subsequently exhibited at the Paris Exposition of 1878.

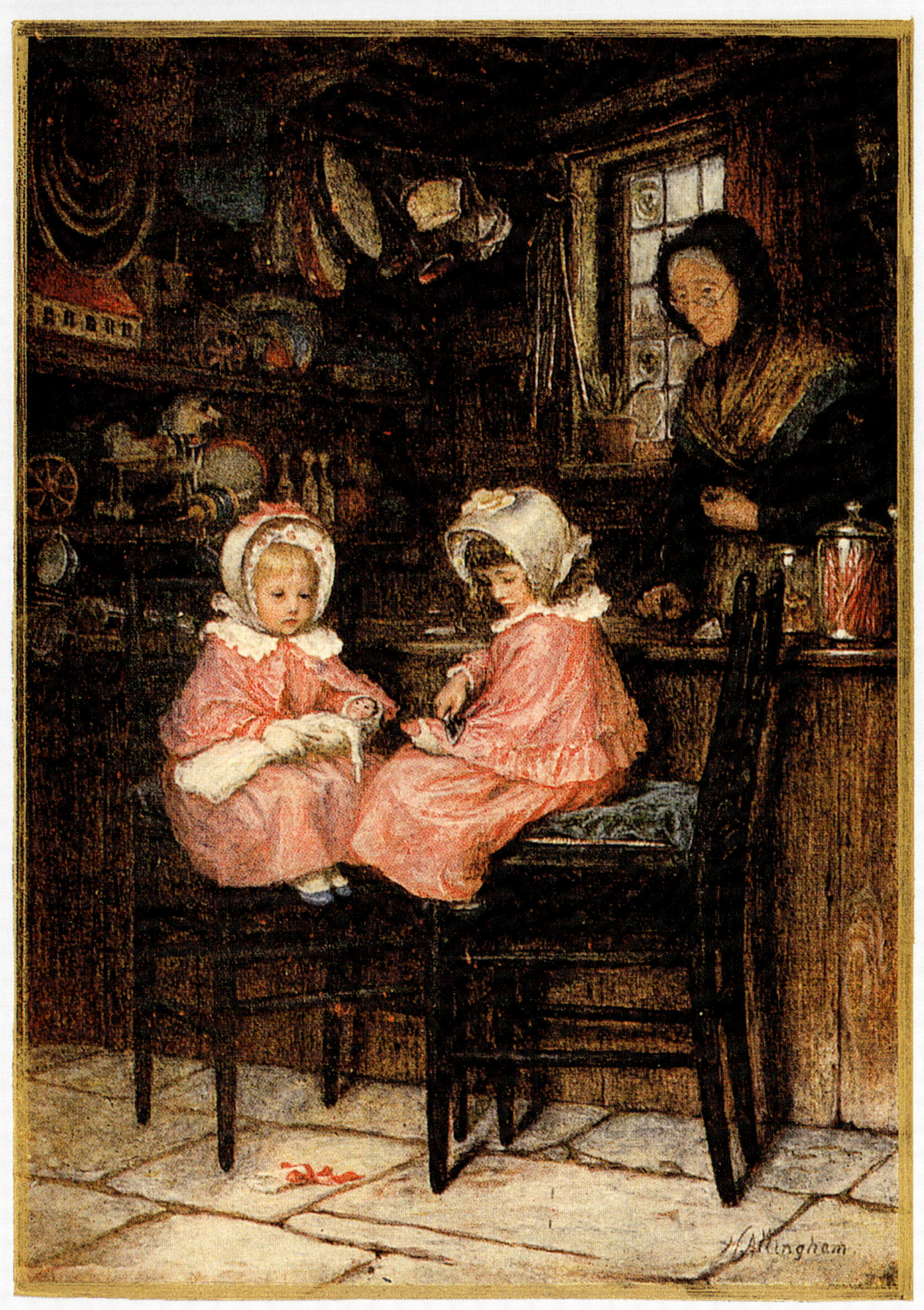

HELEN ALLINGHAM'S WORLD

The word 'idyllic' suggests itself for the title of this book because of the particular aspect of her country which Mrs. Allingham chose to portray. As regards both life and landscape her work is – and was, throughout her career – a mirror of halcyon days. If sickness intrudes on a single occasion, it is in its convalescent stage; if she paints old age, it is in a 'Haven of Rest' – the Royal Hospital Chelsea, near her home for the first years of her married life. In Mrs. Allingham's world the wandering pedlar finds a ready market for her wares, the tramp assistance by the wayside. In both life and landscape it is a portrayal of youth rejoicing in its youth. This healthiness, happiness and joy of life, coupled with an idyllic beauty, reveals itself in every figure in Mrs. Allingham's story, so that even the drudgery of rural life is made to appear as a task to be envied.

The same joyous and happy note is to be found in her landscapes. Every scene is

> Full in the smile of the blue firmament.

One feels that

> Every flower
> Enjoys the air it breathes.

Rain, wind, or lowering skies find no place in any of them, but each calls forth the expression

> What a day
> To sun one and do nothing!

HELEN ALLINGHAM, 1848-1926

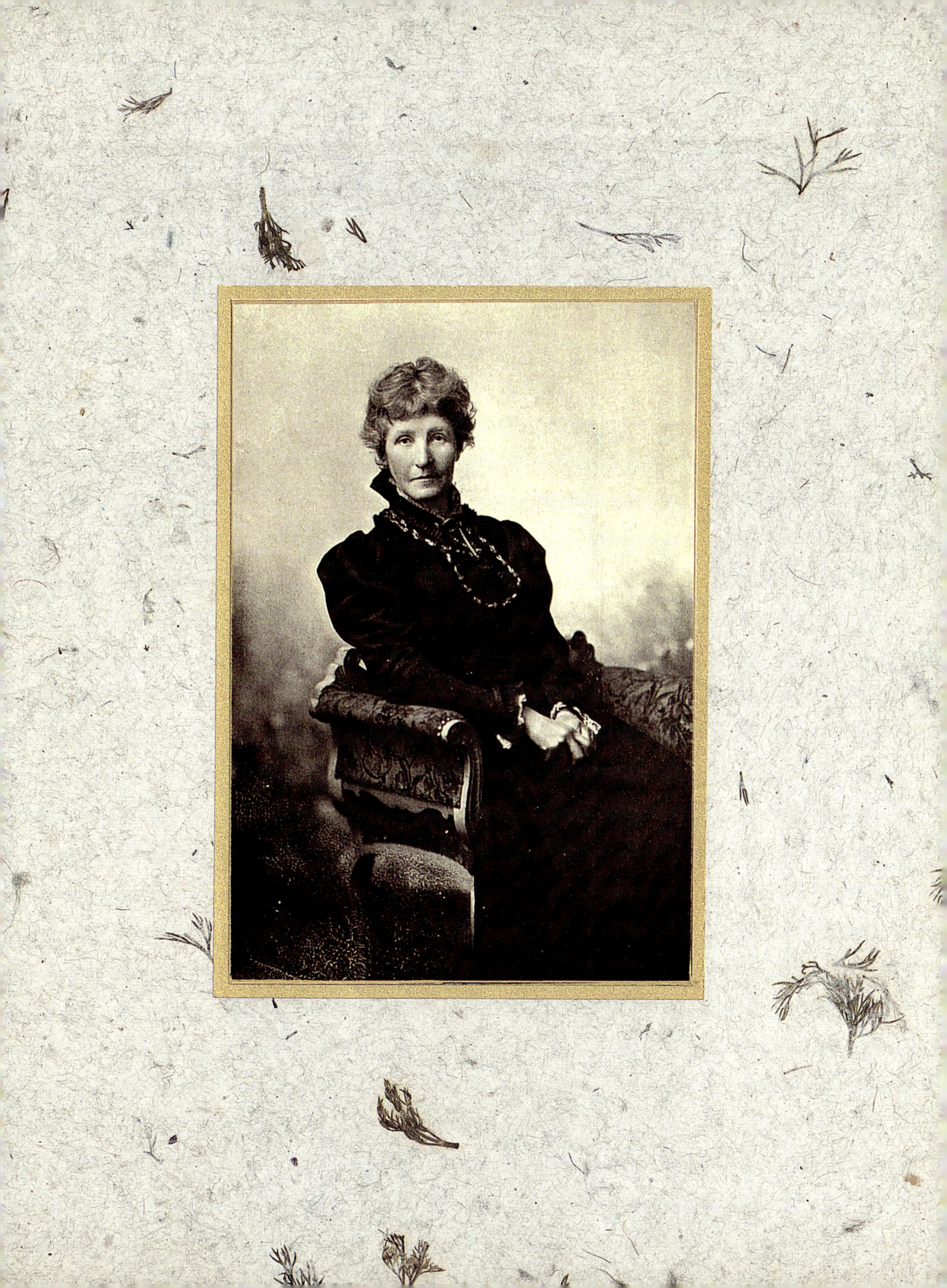

She made no attempt to depict the sterner effects of landscape of which earlier English painters were so fond. With the rough steeps of Hindhead at her door, Helen Allingham's feet almost invariably turned towards the lowlands and the reposeful forms of the distant South Downs. Cottages, farmsteads and flower gardens were her choice in preference to dales, crags and fells.

In exercising this choice, she certainly catered for the happiness of the greater number, as this cry of the urban worker, long confined to the city, indicates:

> 'Tis very sweet to look into the fair
> And open face of heaven?

And Robert Browning in his 'Home Thoughts from Abroad' gives whole-hearted expression to the homesickness of the exile – even though he was living in Italy, where many would think the offerings of Nature were far more beautiful than those of his native land.

> Oh! to be in England
> Now that April's here!
> . . . .

THE CLOTHES-LINE
painted 1879

This is another of the artist's early works. Contemporary criticisms of this watercolour were that 'the woman still smacks... too much of the studio, and she is a lady-like model, certainly not the type one would expect to see hanging out the washing of a... humble wardrobe as in this case'. This comment was justified: the woman was a Mrs Stewart, who, with her husband, sat for Helen Allingham for years. They had for a long time been neighbours in London and this picture is typical of the work produced by the artist before she moved to the house at Sandhills, near Witley, in Surrey.

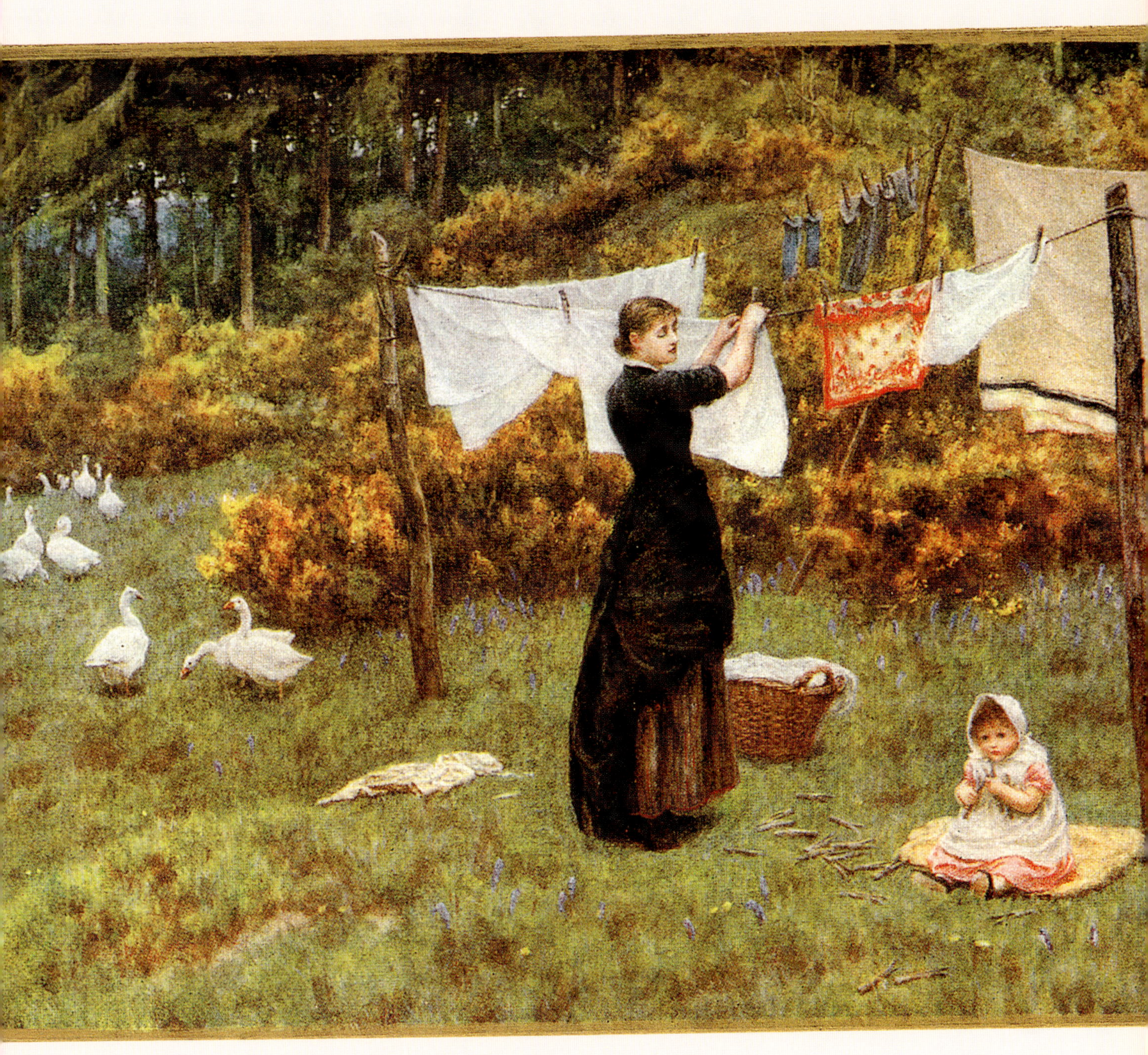

All will be gay when noontide wakes anew
The Buttercups, the little children's dower,
Far brighter than this gaudy melon flower!

It is to this longing that Mrs. Allingham's idyll makes its most profound appeal.

The popularity of her paintings also owes much to the advances in colour reproduction which took place in the course of her working life. During the last decades of the nineteenth century, the development of what was known as the three-colour process enabled coloured representations of an artist's work to be made available to the public in a way that had not up till then been possible. Until that time, most self-respecting painters had been understandably reluctant to allow any colour reproductions of their work to be made except by processes whose cost and complexity necessarily kept numbers small. A demonstration of the three-colour process persuaded Mrs. Allingham to permit her paintings to be published in this way. So it was that a leap forward in science enabled reproductions of her water-colours to be offered to thousands who had not known them previously.

Before embarking on a description of Mrs. Allingham's career, it might interest the reader to know a little of the difficulties that faced a woman who wished to pursue a career in Art in the late Victorian period. By the beginning of the twentieth century, woman painters were in such profusion

❤❤

THE WALLER OAK, COLESHILL
painted 1902

Coleshill, where the tree stood, was then a 'woody hamlet' near Amersham, a mile or two from Chalfont St Giles in Buckinghamshire. This venerable oak was named after Edmund Waller, the English poet (1606–87), born at Coleshill, who is supposed to have composed much of his work in the shade of this oak.

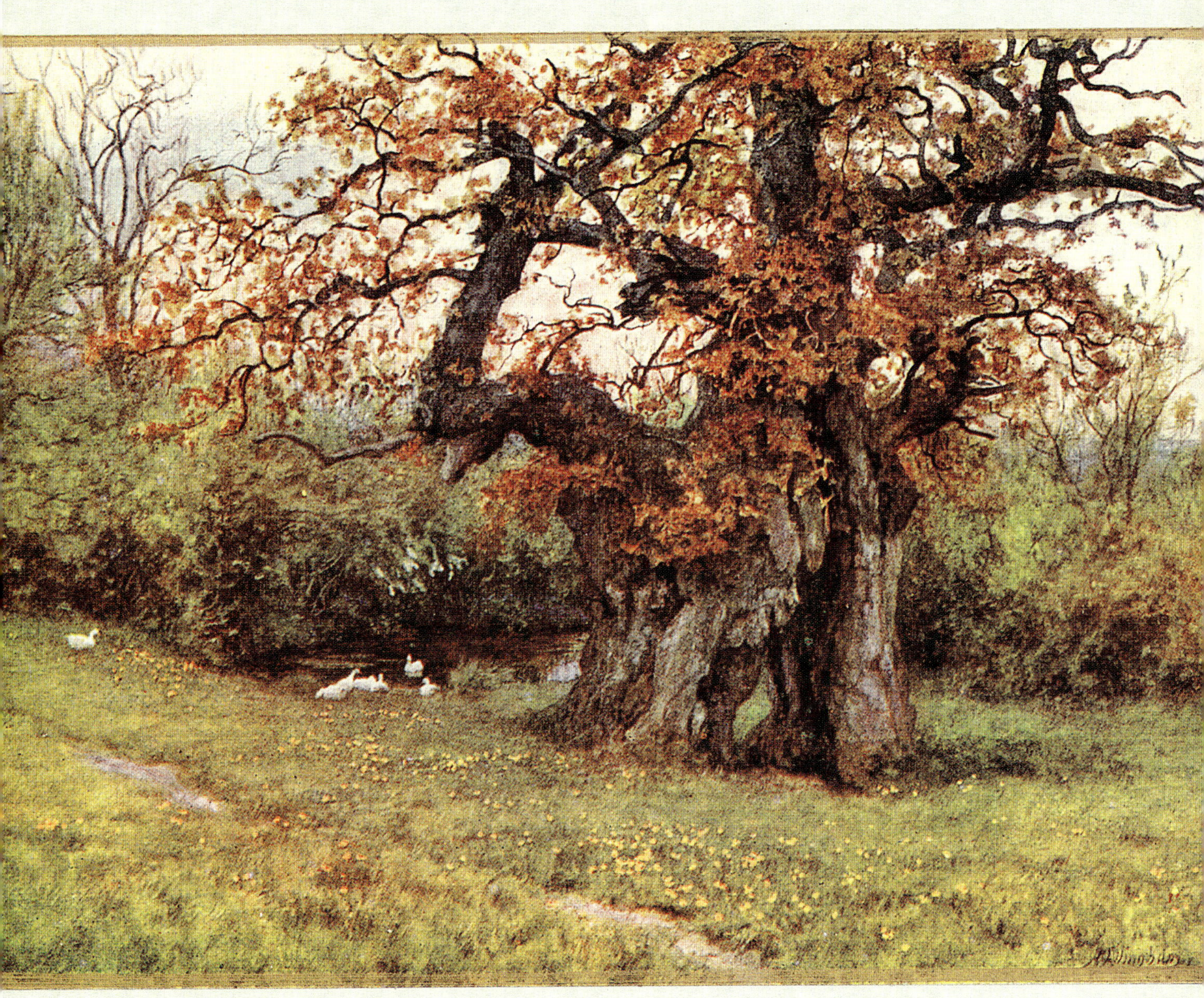

(some four thousand women described themselves thus in the census of 1901) that it is easy to forget that the female artist worthy of a place amongst the foremost of her male counterparts, was a creature of recent development. As late as 1850 it could fairly be said that the majority of these ladies owed both their practice and their place in Art to the fact of their fathers or husbands having been engaged in that profession.

History has recorded little concerning the women who worked in the early days of English Art. A largely forgotten artist called Lavinia Teerlinck is known to have died rich and respected, having received in her prime a higher salary than the great Holbein, portrait painter to Henry VIII; towards the end of Miss Teerlinck's life Queen Elizabeth granted her a quarterly wage of £41. A century later Mary Beale earned £200 a year from her brush, charging £5 for a head and £10 for a half-length.

Midway through the eighteenth century we come across a great and unique event in the annals of Female Art – the election of two ladies to the Royal Academy, in the persons of Angelica Kauffmann – who was one of the

IN THE HAYLOFT
painted 1880

*This was practically the last watercolour which the artist based on
earlier pictures executed in black and white as book illustrations.
The story is from* Deborah's Drawer *by Eleanor Grace O'Reilly, for
which Helen Allingham had made nine drawings in 1870, at a time
when she was so inexperienced in drawing on wood that in more than
one instance her signature appears turned the wrong way. George Bell,
the publisher of the book, subsequently commissioned a watercolour
based on the story, which was to be a companion to 'The Young
Customers' (see page 9). The twins in the picture are orphans. They hide
in the hayloft to reminisce about their dead mother –
a popular Victorian theme.*

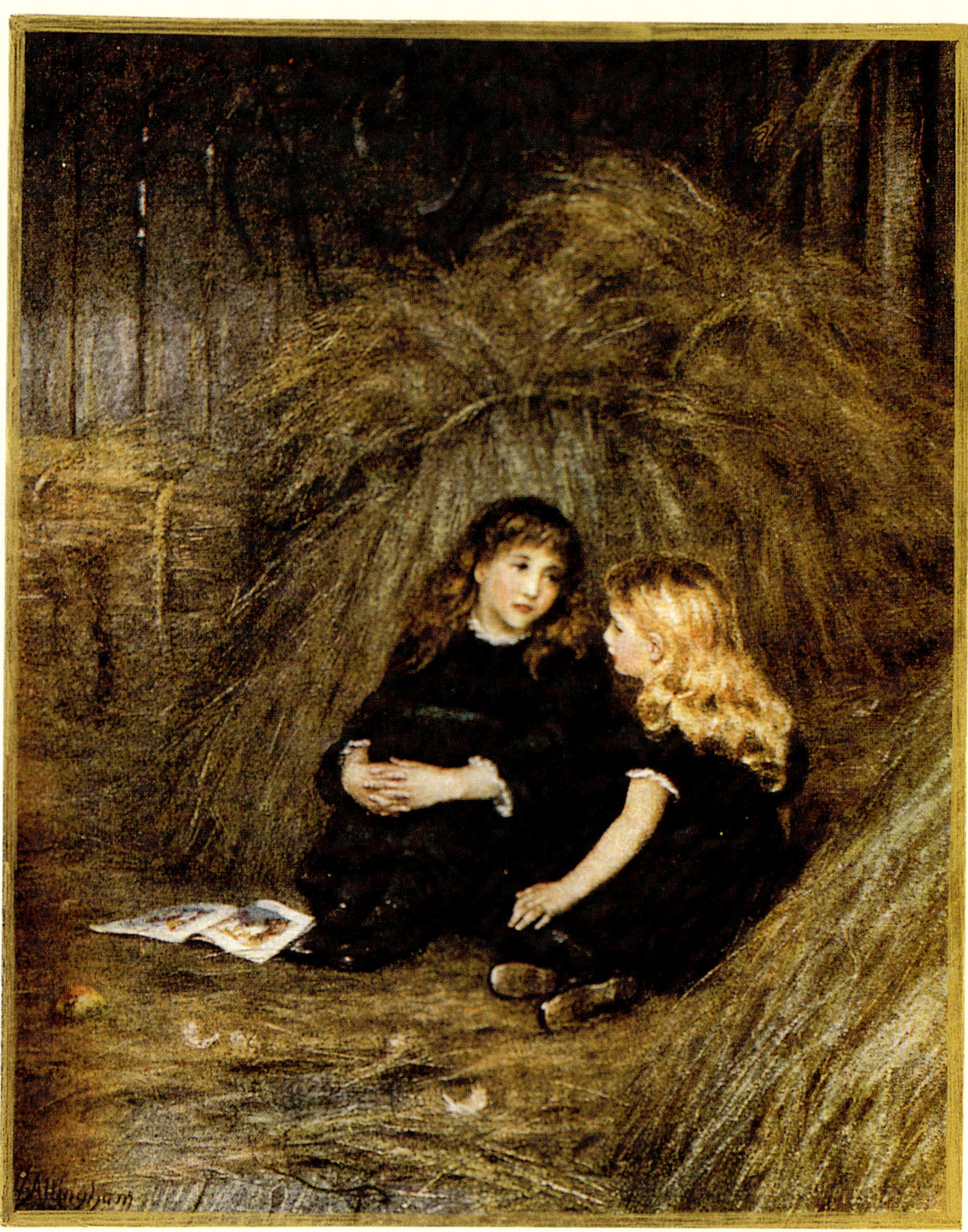

original signatories of the petition to George III, asking him to found an Academy, and who therefore gained admittance on the granting of that privilege – and Mary Moser.

The only other female artists who flit across the stage during the latter half of that century are Frances Reynolds, sister of Sir Joshua Reynolds, first President of the Academy; and Maria Cosway, wife of the miniaturist Richard Cosway, court painter to the Prince Regent. These two kept up the tradition of women always being connected with Art by parentage or marriage.

The admission of women to the Royal Academy Schools in 1860 – an event with which Helen Allingham's aunt, Laura Herford, was closely connected, as we shall see – must have had much to do not only with increasing the number of women artists, but with raising the standard of their work. Within thirty years they had firmly established their right to be considered alongside the men, by carrying off many of the most important awards. The first female gold medallist was Miss Louisa Starr (later Madame Canziani) and she was followed by Miss Jessie Macgregor, a niece of Alfred Hunt, whose influence on Helen Allingham's career will be considered later in this book. By the turn of the century the Royal Female School of Art, the Slade School and Schools of Art everywhere throughout the country were engaged in swelling the ranks of the profession.

Nevertheless, with the two exceptions already named, election to membership of the Royal Academy had been barred to ladies since its foundation. The day when their talent in oil painting, or any other art medium, would be recognised by Academic honours was a long time coming. Marcus Huish R.A. was presumably not voicing the general opinion of his fellow Academicians when he wrote with enthusiasm of the talents of the new generation of women artists, and lamented their treatment at the hands of the powerful men of their profession:

❦❦

THE CONVALESCENT

painted 1879

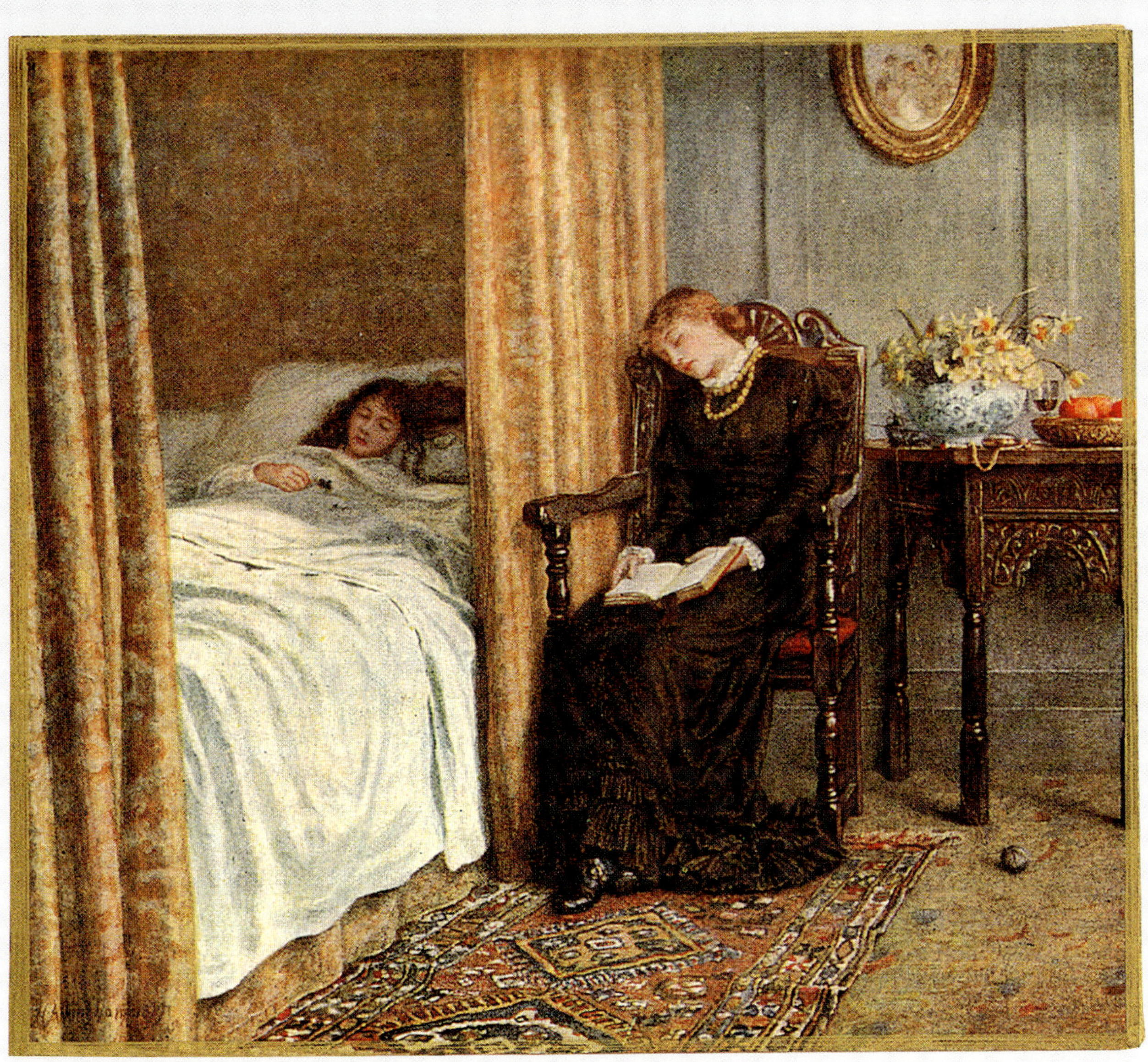

This invasion of womankind into Art, which also showed itself in a remarkable way in poetry and fiction, came as a delightful surprise, as a breath of fresh and sweet-scented air after the heavy atmosphere which had hung over Art in the previous generation...The endeavours of women in what is termed very erroneously the higher branch of the profession have not as yet received the reward that is their due. Placed at the Royal Academy under practically the same conditions as the male sex whilst under tuition, their pictures, when they mount from the Schools in the basement to the Exhibition Galleries on the first floor of Burlington House, carry with them no further possibility of reward, even although they hold the pride of place there.

Not all the artistic institutions were so entrenched in their prejudices. Both the Royal Society and the Royal Institute of Painters in Water Colours admitted women whom they deemed worthy exponents of the art.

It seems likely that the growth in popularity of water-colour paintings and the burgeoning number of successful women artists were closely connected. Certainly Marcus Huish thought so:

The practice of water-colour art would appear to appeal especially to womankind, as not only are the constituents which go to its making of a more agreeable character than those of oil, but the whole machinery necessary for its successful production is more compact and capable of adaptation to the ordinary house. The very methods employed have a certain daintiness about them which coincides with a lady's delicacy. The work does not necessitate hours of standing, with evil-smelling paints, in a large top-lit studio, but can be effected seated, in any living room which contains a

❤❤

THE RABBIT HUTCH
painted 1880

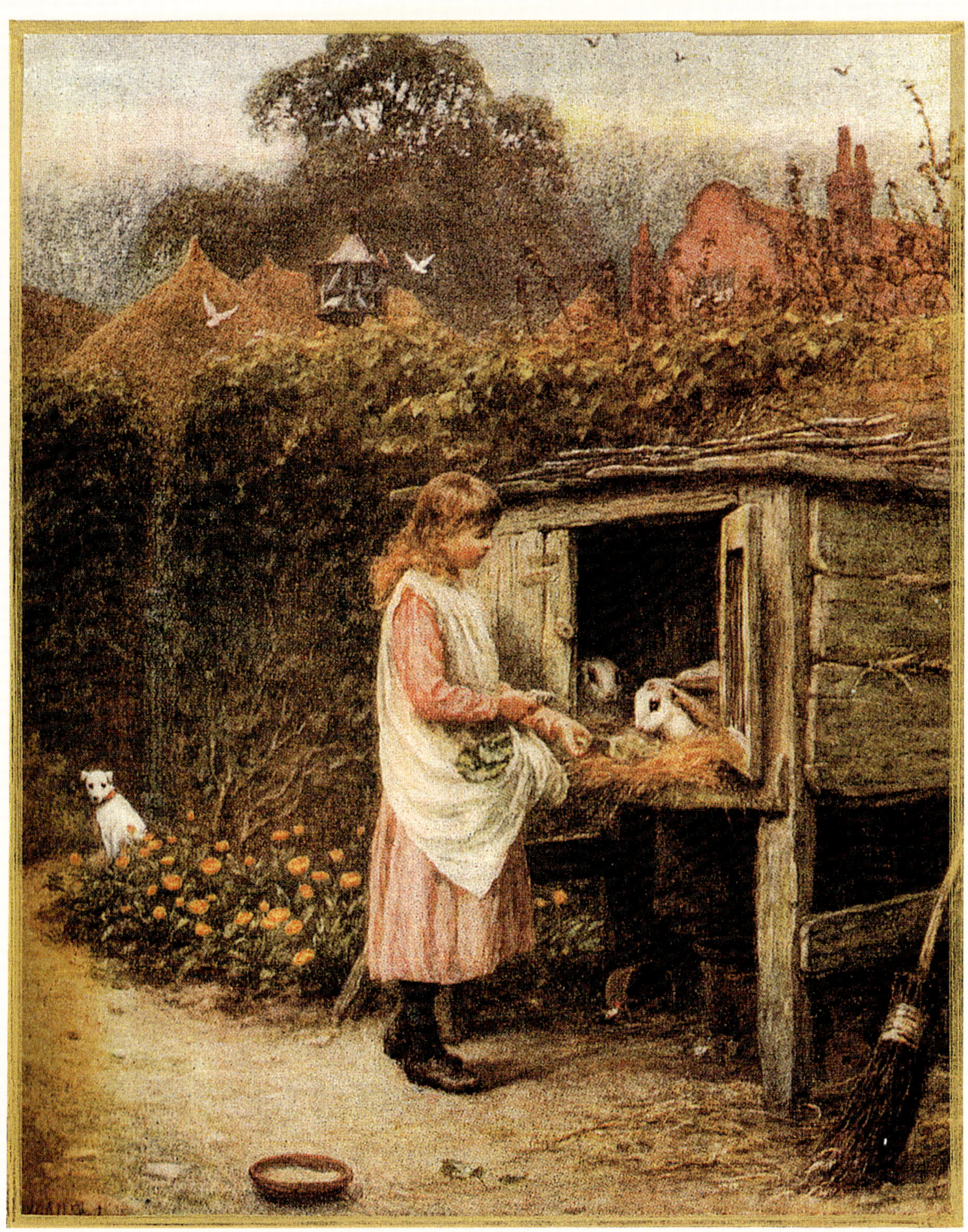

window of sufficient size. There is no need to leave all the materials about while the canvasses dry, and no preliminary setting of palettes and subsequent cleaning off.

Yet in spite of this the water-colour art during the first century of its existence was practised almost solely by the male sex, and it was not until the middle of the Victorian reign that a few women came on to the scene and at once showed themselves the equals of the male sex, not only so far as proficiency but originality was concerned. In the case of no one of these was there any imitation of following of a master; but each struck out for herself what was, if not a new line, certainly a presentation of an old one in a novel form.

The guise in which Helen Allingham presented that 'line' is the subject of the following pages.

COTTAGE AT CHIDDINGFOLD
painted 1889

Helen Allingham became justly famous for her paintings of picturesque cottages. This one was in the old hamlet of Chiddingfold in Kent. At the time of painting, Cherry Tree Cottage was the village milk shop and was, at least at certain times of the day, a busy and prosperous place.

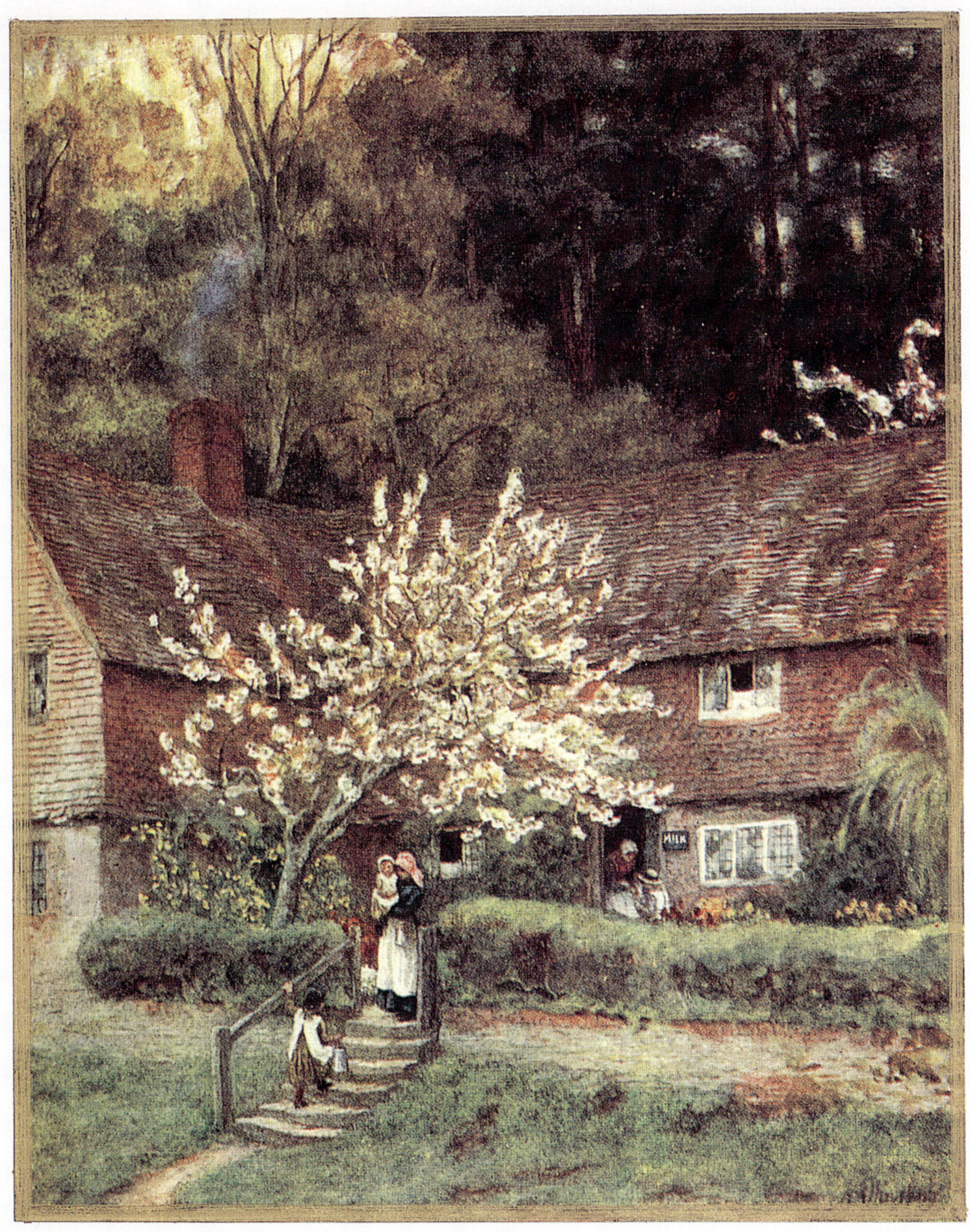

EARLY CAREER

Mrs. Allingham, whose maiden name was Helen Paterson, was born on September 26, 1848, near Burton-on-Trent, Derbyshire, where her father, Alexander Henry Paterson, M.D., had a medical practice. As her name implies, she was of Scottish descent on the paternal side. A year after her birth her family removed to Altrincham in Cheshire, where her father died, suddenly, in 1862, of diphtheria, caught in attending a patient.

This unforeseen blow broke up the Cheshire household and the widow shortly afterwards wended her way with her young family to Birmingham, where the young artist spent the next few years, the most impressionable of her life, in surroundings which cannot have influenced her in the direction of Art of any kind.

Scribbling out of her head on any material she could lay hold of (not even sparing the polished surfaces of the Victorian furniture) had been her chief pleasure as a child; and as she grew older she drew from Nature with interest and ease, especially during family visits to Kenilworth and other country and seaside places. Some friends in Birmingham started a drawing club which met each month at houses of the different members and the young student

❦❦

NIGHT-JAR LANE, WITLEY
painted 1887

One of those steep self-made roads which the passage of the seasons rather than of man has furrowed and deepened in the surrounding woods. The lane is named after the elusive bird of that name, described by Gilbert White as 'a wonderful and curious creature' which lets out its 'jar' or note exactly at the close of the day. White assures his readers that, in summer, he always heard the bird at the same time as the report of the gun in Portsmouth Harbour which heralded the end of another day.

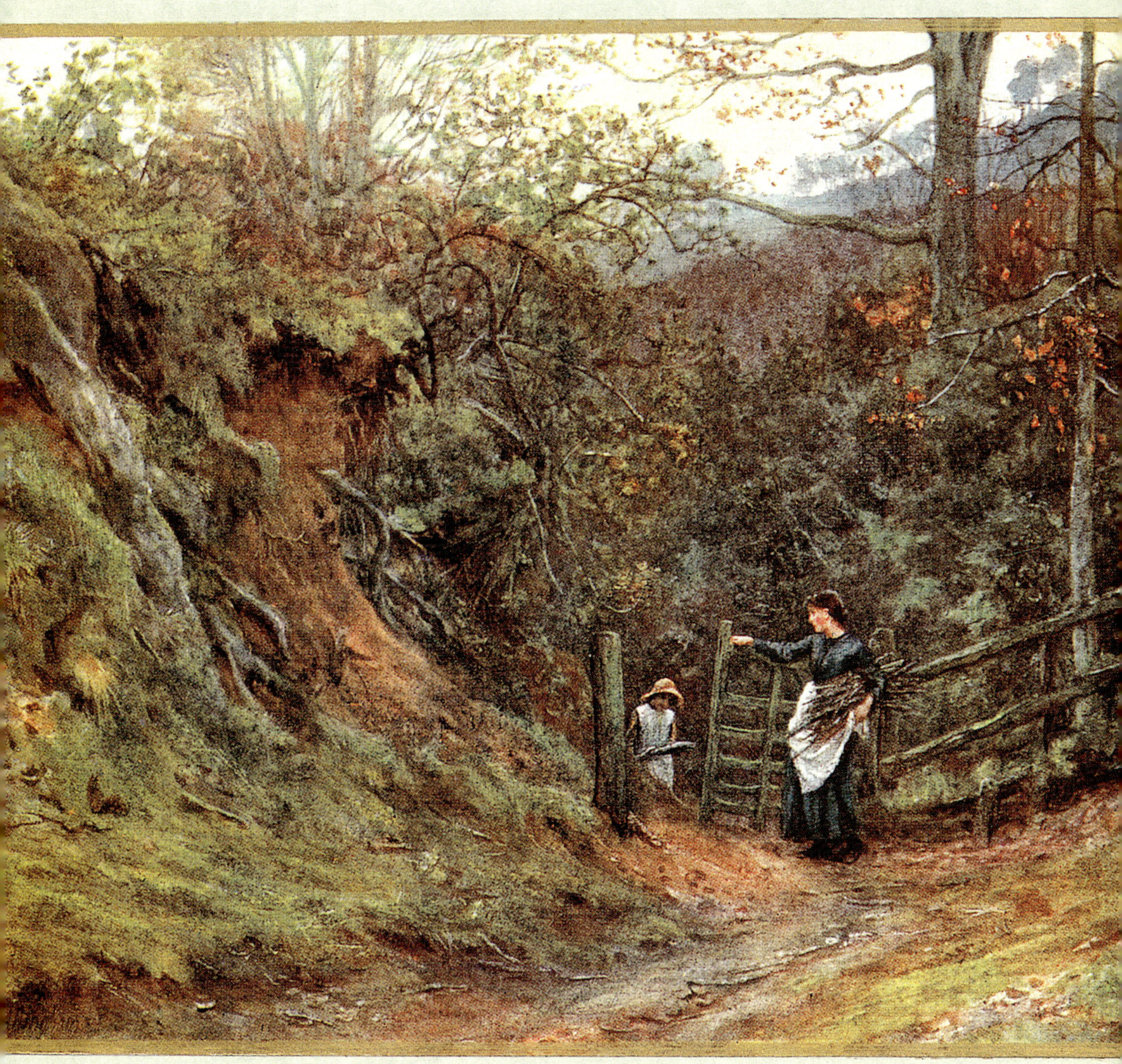

was invited to join it. Subjects were fixed upon and drawings were shown and discussed at each meeting. More good resulted from this than might have been expected, for some of the members were collectors of fine examples in Art, which were also seen and considered at the meetings. Helen Paterson, finding that her pen-and-ink productions were more satisfactory than her colour attempts, came to hope that she might gradually qualify herself for book illustration, instead of earning a living by teaching, as she at first anticipated would be her lot.

Two influences greatly helped the girl in her artistic desires at this time.

Helen Paterson's mother's sister, Laura Herford, had taken up Art as a profession. Although her name does not often appear in Exhibition records, the sisterhood of artists owes her a very enduring debt. For to her was due the opening of the Royal Academy Schools to women, which she obtained through another's slip of the tongue, aided by a successful subterfuge.

Lord Lyndhurst, at a Royal Academy banquet, in singing the praises of that institution, claimed that its schools offered free tuition to all Her Majesty's subjects. Within a few days he received from Miss Herford a letter pointing out the inaccuracy of this statement, inasmuch as tuition was only given to the male, and not to the female sex, which comprised the majority of Her Majesty's subjects. She therefore appealed to him to use his influence with the Government to obtain the removal of the restriction. He did so, and the Government, on addressing Sir Charles Eastlake, the President of the Royal Academy, found him altogether in sympathy with such a reform. He replied to the Government that there was no written law against the admission of women, and after an interview with the lady he connived at a drawing of hers being sent in as a test of her capability for admission as a probationer,

♥♥

APPLE AND PEAR BLOSSOM
painted 1901

Spring scene in an Isle of Wight lane.

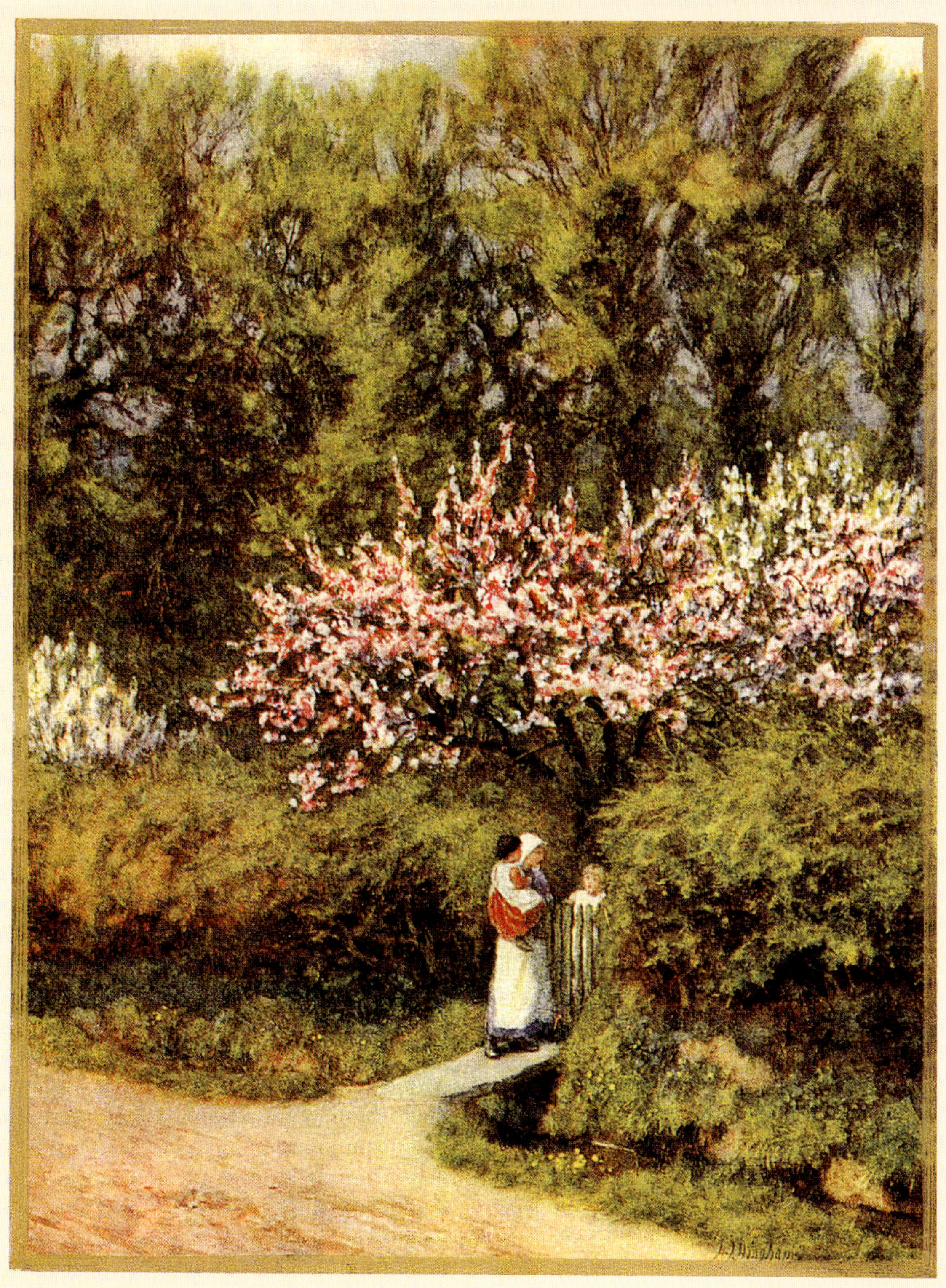

under the initials merely of her Christian names. A few days subsequently a notification that he had passed the test and obtained admission arrived at her home addressed to A. L. Herford, Esq.

There was of course an outcry when the lady presented herself in answer to the summons to execute a drawing in the presence of the Keeper; and her insistence that she should stay and do this was vehemently combated by the Council to whom it was referred. But the President demonstrated the absurdity of the situation, and so strongly advocated the untenability of the position that the door was opened once and for all to female students. This strong-willed lady constituted herself Art-adviser-in-chief to young Helen Paterson from the time of her father's death.

The other influence under which the budding artist came at this critical period was that of a capable and sympathetic master at Birmingham, Mr. Raimbach, the head of the Birmingham School of Design. A teacher born not made, he saw and fostered whatever gifts were to be found in his pupils. It was he who encouraged Helen Paterson to go to London for wider study, in the hope of gaining entrance into the Academy Schools, and taking up Art as a profession under her aunt's auspices. The future Mrs. Allingham duly passed into the Academy Schools in April 1867.

During the first year or two there she worked in the antique school, where the concentration on the study of drawing and the proportions of the figure, with some anatomy, precluded the thought of painting. When raised to the painting school she, like many another capable student then as now, was at first driven hither and thither by the apparently contradictory advice she

❤❤

THE OLD YEW TREE
painted 1903

The sad yew tree is seen
Still with the black cloak round his ancient wrongs.
William Allingham

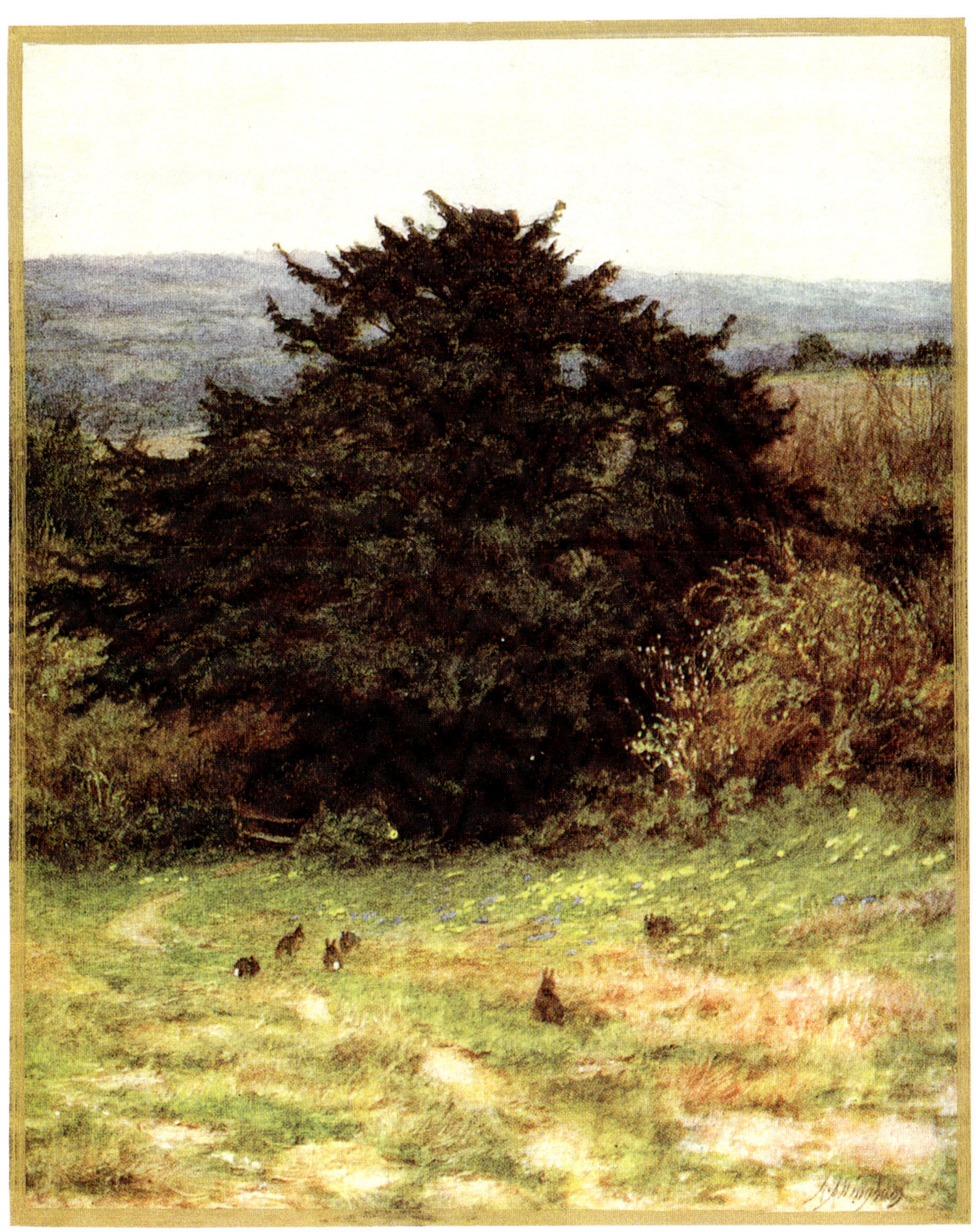

received from her masters. For one month she was under a visitor with strongly defined ideas in one direction, and the next under someone else who was equally assertive in another, and it was some time before she could draw upon all these sources to form her own opinions. But she received help and kindness from all, and, as she gratefully remembered, from none more so than from the great John Everett Millais, who had made his name as a founding member of the pre-Raphaelite brotherhood, but had moved away from them to execute magnificent portraits of prominent men, and to become one of the most brilliant woodcut designers of his generation. Millais could in a minute or two impart something which she never afterwards forgot, whilst as a beginner she also found the encouragement of many other established artists most stimulating.

Another artist who was a life-long adviser and the kindest of friends was Briton Riviere, eight years Miss Paterson's senior and an established painter of figures and animals – he had first exhibited at the Royal Academy in 1864 and became a full member of the Academy in 1881.

With Mr. Riviere and his family an intimacy began even in Miss Paterson's student days. An invitation to stay with them at St Andrews in the summer of 1872 inaugurated her first serious work from Nature. Mr. Riviere's approval of the result helped to dissipate a certain despondency and fear which had sprung up in the young artist's mind as regards her colour powers. Just prior to this visit she had been taken by an old friend of the family to Rome, where she had worked assiduously at Nature, but been little satisfied

In Witley Village
painted 1884

This drawing was in the Fine Art Society's Exhibition of 1886, the catalogue stating that the cottage had disappeared in the spring of 1885, pulled down by its owner. Birket Foster also mourned the disappearance of the lovely old building, having at one point contemplated the possibility of reconstructing it in his own grounds.

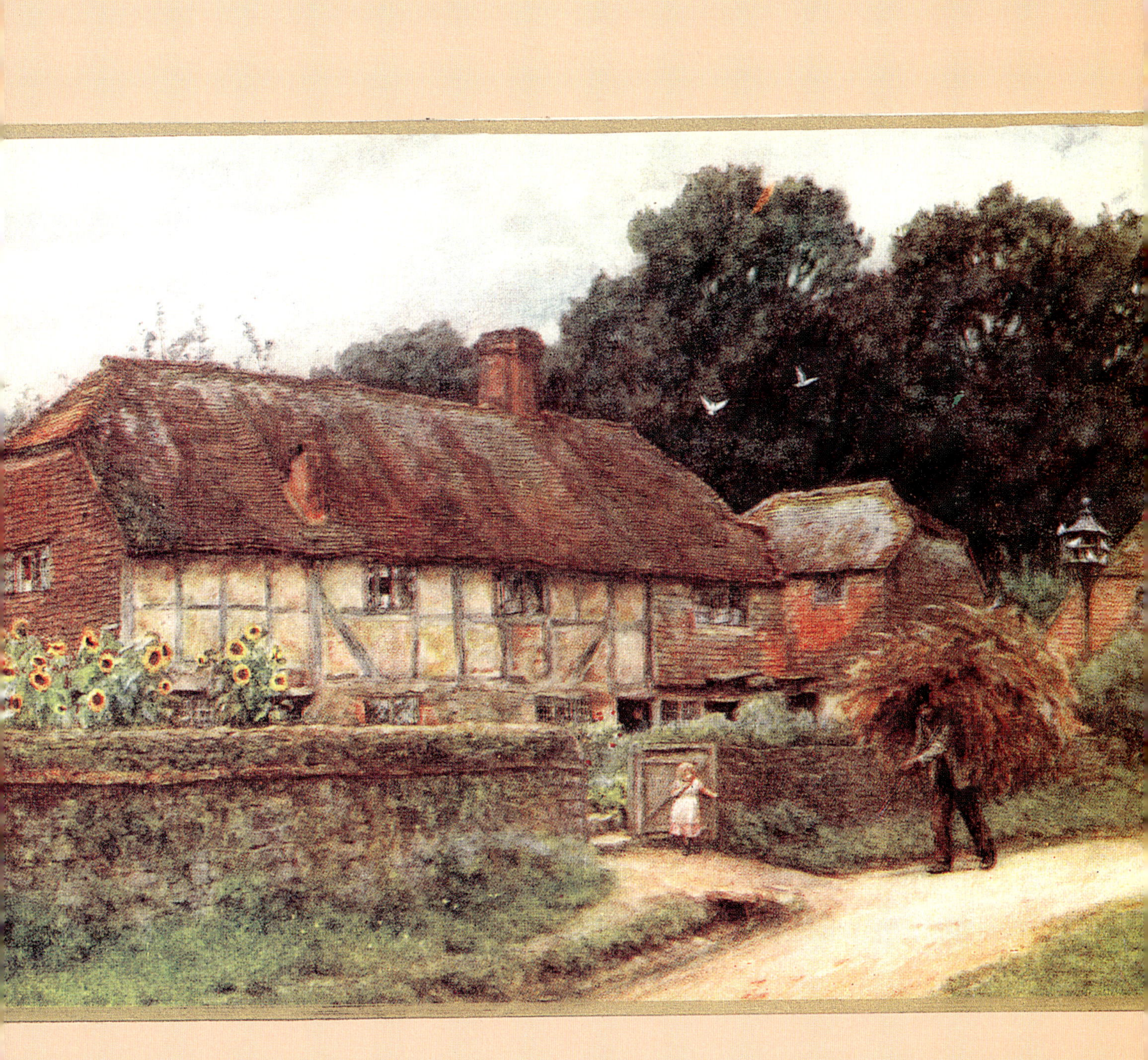

with the result. In St. Andrews things took a happier turn. It was not, however, in the grey houses and streets of this old northern university town, to which she first turned, that her longing eye discovered the true relations between tone and colour, but amongst the sandbanks, seaweed and blue water which fringed its noted golf-links. For the first time she felt happy in attempting to work in a medium other than black and white.

She had by this time fully made up her mind to embark on a career in which she was determined, and was in fact obliged, to earn a living; and as her colour work at present had no market, there was nothing for it but to procure a livelihood by black and white. Wood engraving, although nearing the end of its existence, was still the only medium of cheap illustration. Photography later on came to its aid to a certain extent, but the majority of the original drawings continued to be drawn directly on to the wood block. There were still close upon a hundred wood engravers employed in London, working for the most part under master engravers, into whose hands the publishers of magazines, illustrated periodicals and books entrusted, not only the cutting of the block, but the selection of the artist to make the drawing upon it.

It was to these that Helen Paterson had to look for work, and in the autumn of 1869 she diffidently started upon a round of their offices with a portfolio full of drawings. Employment did not come at once, and the list of seventy names with which she had started had been considerably reduced before, to her great satisfaction, a drawing out of her sheaf was taken by Mr. Joseph Swain, to whom she had an introduction, for submission to the proprietors

❤❤

THE CHILDREN'S TEA
painted 1882

The scene is set in the Allinghams' dining room at Sandhills, Surrey, and portrays their children. The mother tries to pass on a cup of tea but the children's attention is taken by the cat, lapping its milk on the floor. One girl is busy feeding her doll while the other two observe a butterfly.

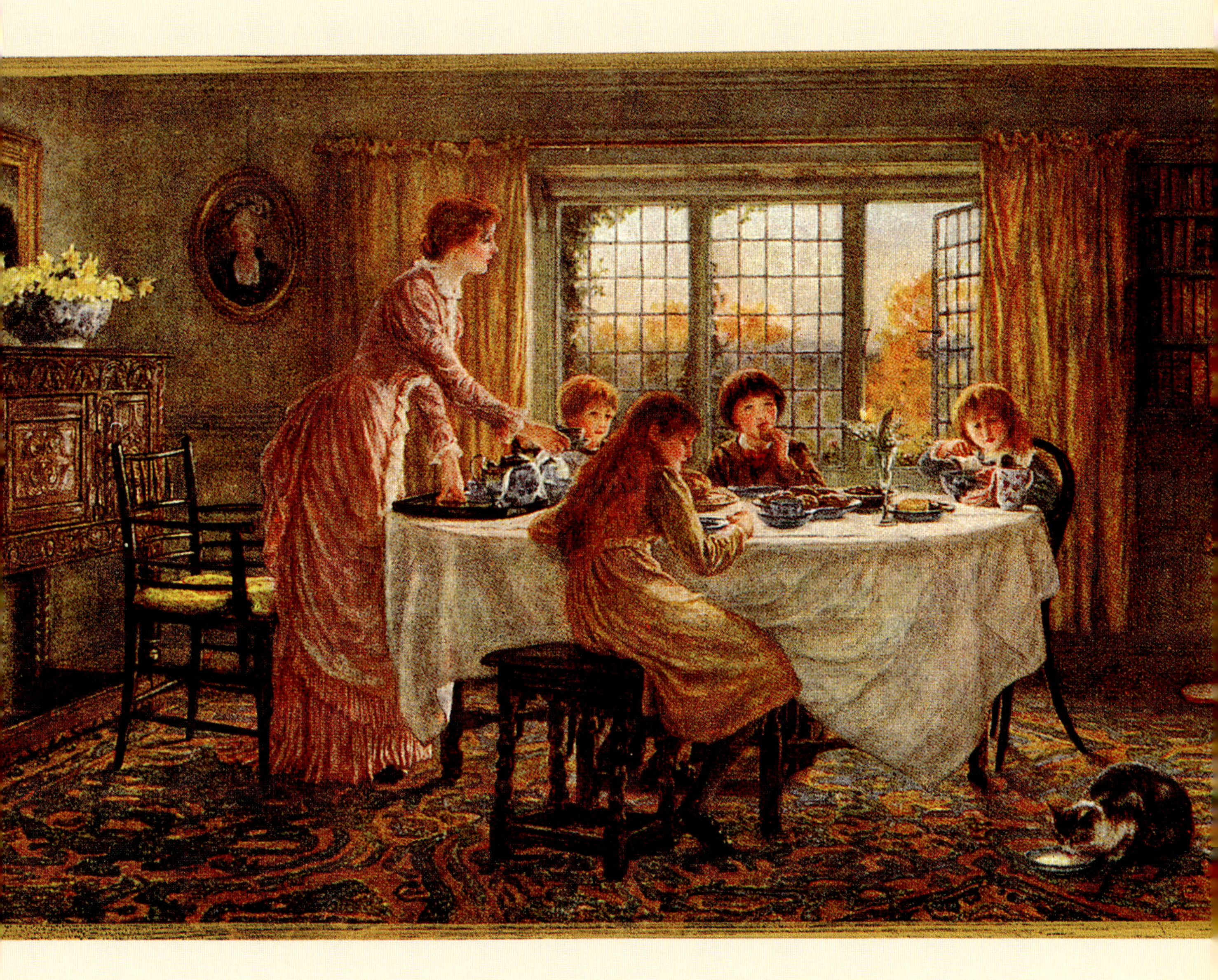

of *Once a Week*. It was accepted, and she copied it on to the wood. Gradually she obtained work for other magazines, including *Little Folks* and *Aunt Judy*.

The first alteration of any magnitude of the custom of the artist having to look to the engraver for work, occurred when the *Graphic* newspaper was started in the year 1870. Mr. W. L. Thomas, to whom the credit of this improvement in the status of the worker in black and white was due, was himself an artist and a member of the Institute of Painters in Water Colours. As such he was not only in touch with, but capable of appreciating the unusual amount of budding talent of abundant promise which was just then presenting itself. The illustrations upon which the success of the *Graphic* mainly depended were not the product of a formulated system, working in a groove, where blocks were served out to artists as to a machine, without any regard to their appropriateness for the particular piece of work. Artists of ability, whose names were later to be found amongst the most noted in the Academic roll, were selected for a particular illustration that suited them, and were well paid for it. The public was not only astonished at, but grateful for, the result, and showed their appreciation by at once placing the *Graphic* in the high position which it deserved.

Helen Paterson was fortunate enough to be brought into touch with Mr. Thomas shortly after the first appearance of the paper and to obtain a place on its staff which she retained until her marriage in 1874. It was indeed a godsend to her, for it meant not only regular work but handsome pay. Twelve guineas for a full and eight for a half page, and at least one of these a week, meant not merely maintenance, but a reserve against that rainy day which, fortunately, she never had to contend with.

❧❧

PAT-A-CAKE
painted 1884

*This charming domestic scene once again portrays two
of the Allingham children.*

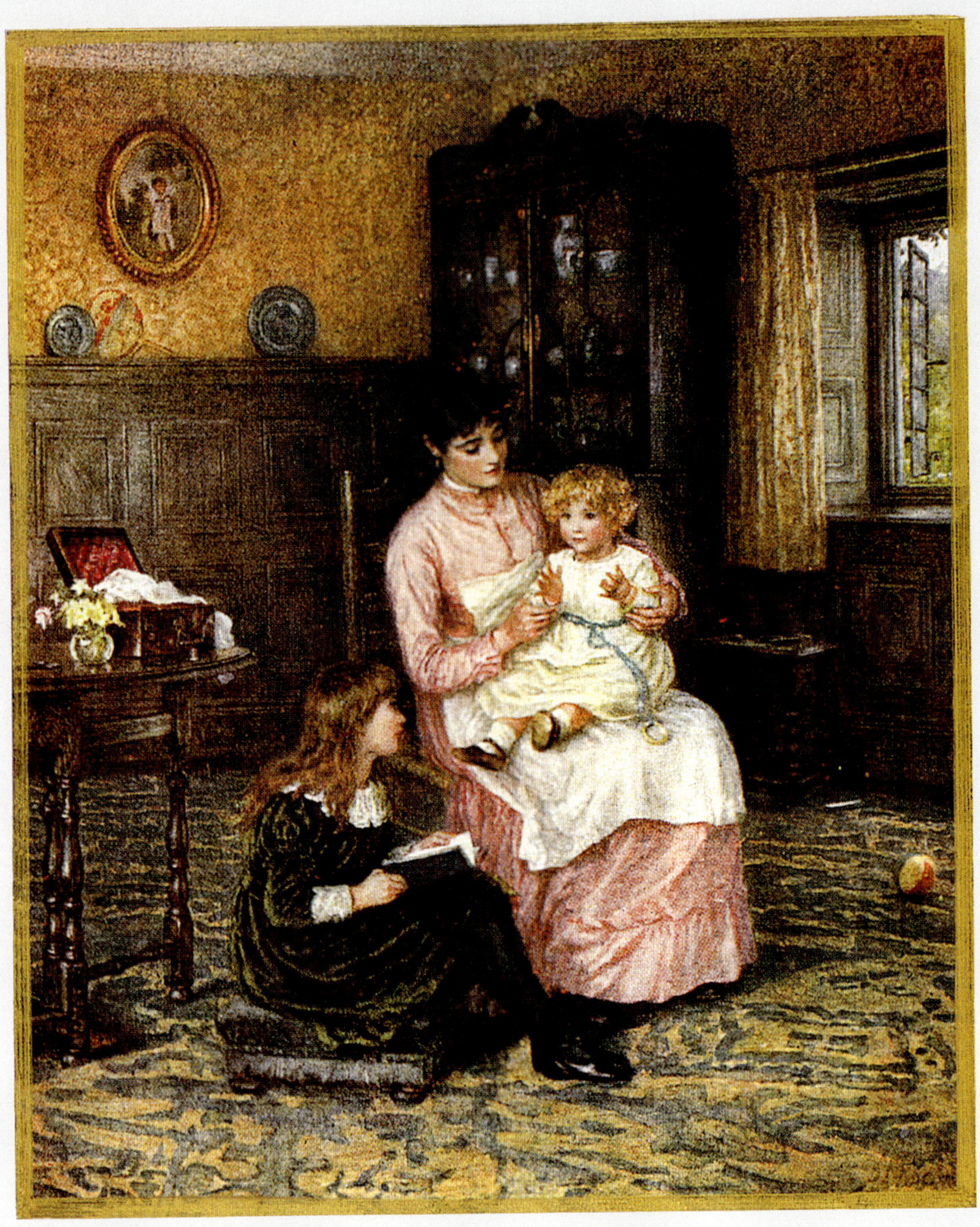

The subjects which she was called upon to produce were diverse in character, but all of them had figures as their main feature. To portray these properly she had to employ regular models, but she also enlisted the aid of her fellow-students, for she was still at the Royal Academy, and her sketch-books of that time, of which she retained many later in life, were full of studies of artists, no few of whom later became celebrated in the world of Art.

Her drawings for the *Graphic* were not always from her own sketches: sometimes they were taken from originals that had been sent to the paper in an embryo condition necessitating entire revision, and sometimes from rapid notes made by artists sent to represent the paper at important functions. But on occasions Miss Paterson was also deputed to attend these, and in consequence underwent some novel experiences for a young girl. A meeting at Mr. Gladstone's, Fashions in the Park, Flower Shows at the Botanical Gardens, Archery with the Toxophilite Society in Regent's Park – these formed the lighter side of her work, the more serious being the illustration of novels by writers of note, which was at the time a new feature in journalism. Amongst those entrusted to her were *Innocent*, by Mrs. Oliphant, and *Ninety-Three*, by Victor Hugo. For the murder trial in the former she had to visit the Central Criminal Court, and through so doing was more accurate than the author, who had not been there and whose work consequently contained several glaring mistakes, such as the prisoner addressing the judge by name.

She was also employed upon a novel by Charles Reade, in conjunction with two other artists. This she undertook with extreme diffidence, for Reade had sent round a circular saying that he greatly disliked having his stories illustrated at all; but as it had to be in this case, he begged to notify that *he* gave *situations*, whilst George Eliot and Anthony Trollope only gave conversations, and he requested that good use should be made of these

❦❦

LESSONS
painted 1885

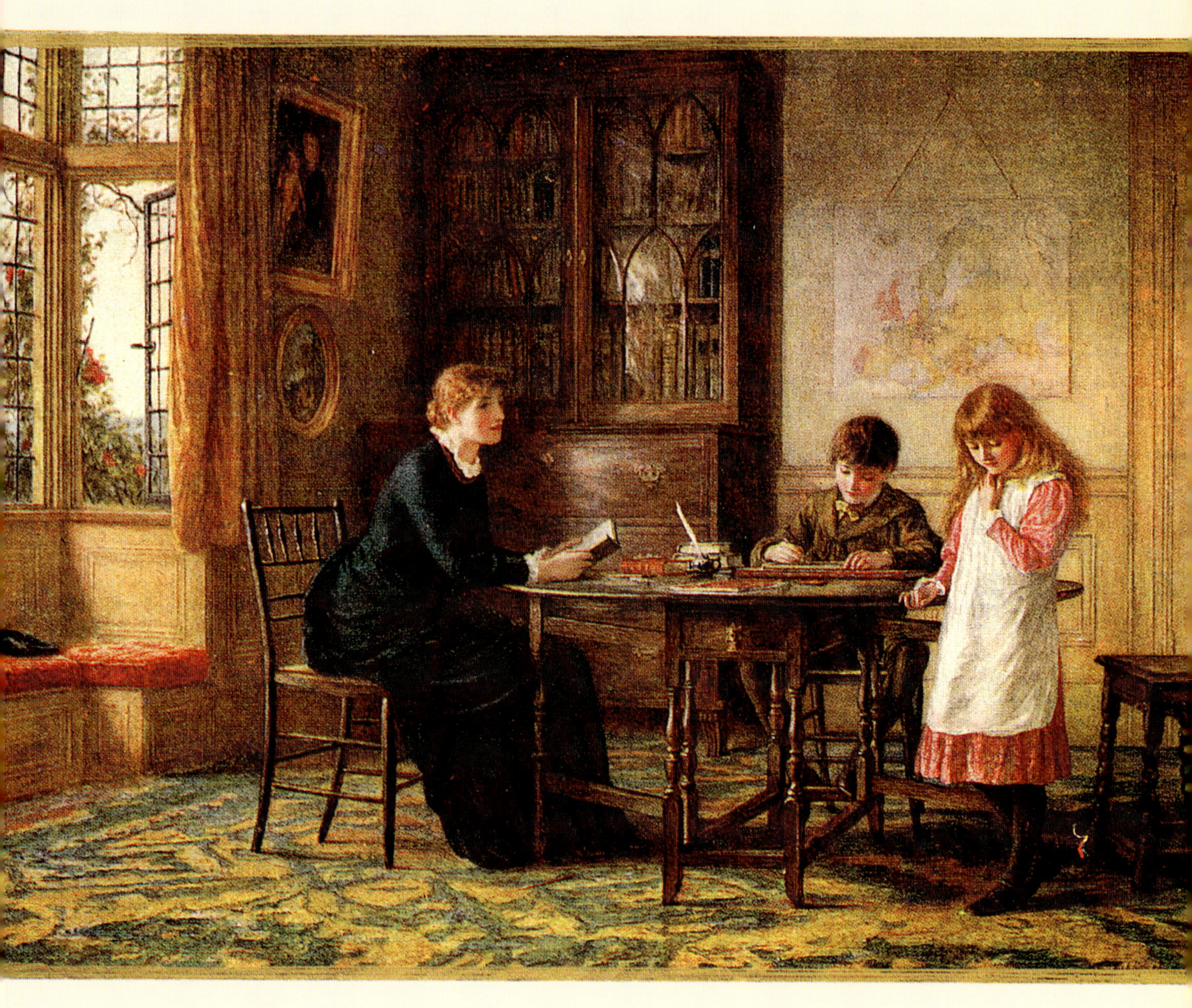

situations. Meeting Helen Allingham some years afterwards, the author paid her the compliment of saying he liked her illustration of the heroine of his story the best of any.

Nor was Miss Paterson entirely dependent upon the *Graphic*, whose illustrations, often given out in a hurry, had to be finished within a matter of hours. She was numbered among the select few who worked for the *Cornhill* magazine, for which she was, through Mr. Swain's kind offices, asked to illustrate Hardy's *Far from the Madding Crowd*, which was at first attributed to George Eliot. The author was fairly complimentary as to the result, although he said it was difficult for two minds to imagine scenes in the same light. Later on she had the pleasant task of illustrating Miss Thackeray's *Miss Angel* in the same magazine. The drawing of Sir Joshua Reynolds asking Angelica to marry him, perhaps the best of the series, was one of the first to be signed with the name of Allingham, by which she was thereafter known.

In the autumn of 1874 Miss Paterson had married William Allingham, the well-known Irish poet, editor of *Fraser's Magazine*. Twenty-four years her senior, he was already an established figure in the literary circles of his birthplace and of London. He had made his name with the collection of verse entitled *Day and Night Songs* (1855), illustrated by Millais and Dante Gabriel Rossetti, who like him were beginning at that time to achieve fame. His greatest work, *Irish Songs and Poems,* was to follow in 1887. It is a tribute to Mr. Allingham's artistic and intellectual capacities that he could count himself the friend of so many of the celebrities in literature, science and art of the middle of the last century, amongst whom may be mentioned Carlyle, Ruskin, Rossetti, Browning and Tennyson. It was to be near the first named that the newly married couple went to reside in Trafalgar Square, Chelsea, where they passed the first seven years of their married life.

❤❤

BUBBLES
painted 1896

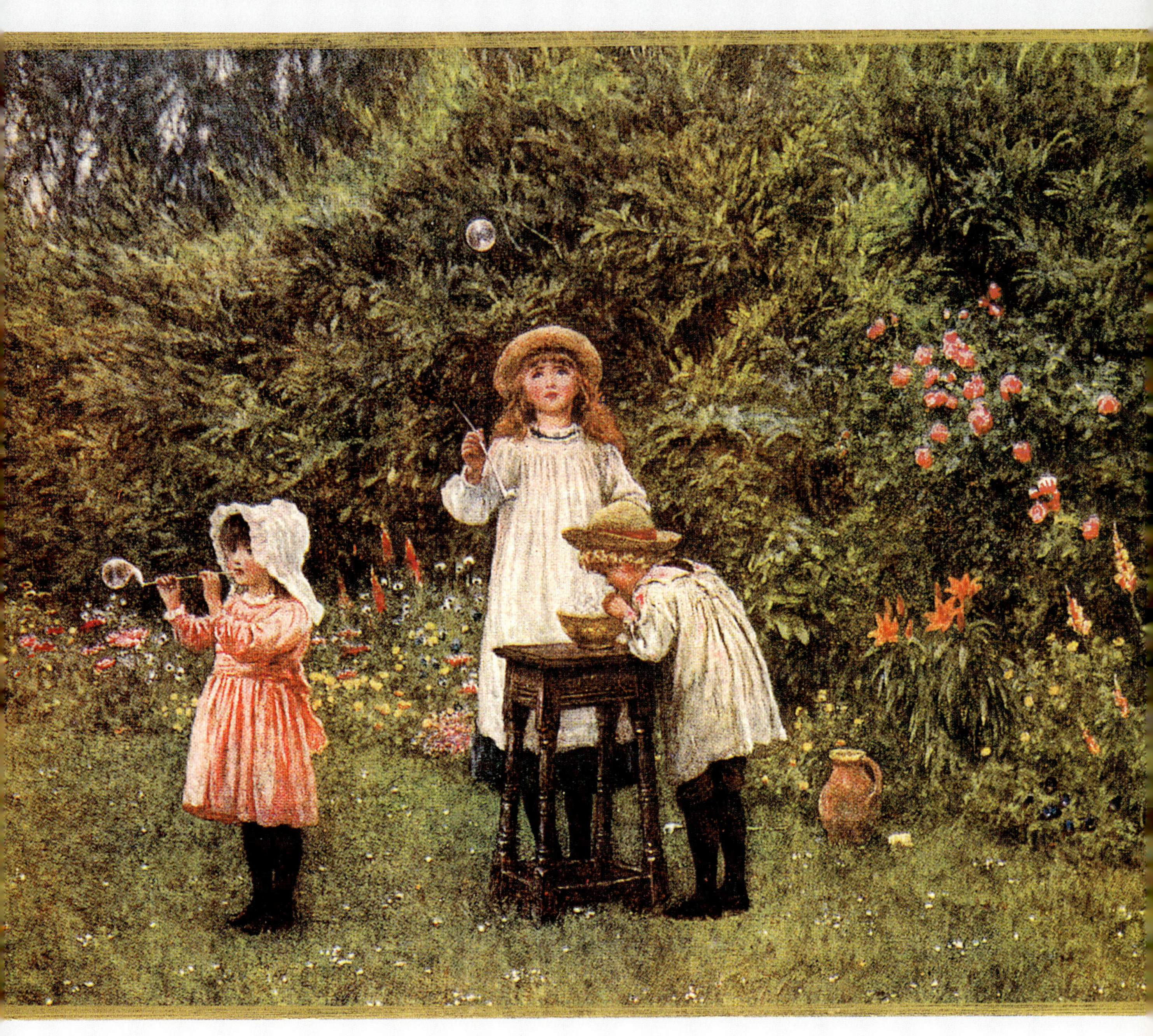

To Carlyle Mrs. Allingham had the privilege of frequent and familiar access during his last years; and when he found that he was not expected to pose to her, and that she had, as he emphatically declared, a real talent for portraiture (the only form of pictorial art in which he took any interest), he became very kind and obliging, and she was able to make nearly a dozen portraits of him in water-colours. An early one, which he declared made him 'look like an old fool,' was painted in the little back garden at No. 5 Cheyne Row, which was not without shade and greenery in the summer time. There, in company with his pet cat 'Tib' and a Paisley churchwarden ('no pipe good for anything,' according to him, 'being get-at-able in England'), he indulged in smoking, the only creature comfort that afforded him any satisfaction. In these portraits he is depicted sitting in his comfortable dressing-gown faded to a dim slaty grey, refusing to wear a gorgeous oriental garment that his admirers had presented to him. An etching of one of these paintings appeared in the *Art Journal* for 1882. Other portraits were painted in the winter of 1878–79, in his long drawing-room with its three windows looking out into the street.

Mr. Allingham had known John Ruskin for many years. His wife's acquaintance began in an interesting fashion at the Old Water-Colour Society. She happened to be there during the Exhibition of 1877 at a time when the room was almost empty. Mr. Ruskin had been looking at her painting of Carlyle and, introducing himself, asked her why she had painted Carlyle like a lamb, when he ought to be painted like a lion, as he was, and whether she would paint the sage as such for him? To this she had to reply that she could only paint him as she saw him, which was certainly not in leonine garb.

One afternoon soon afterwards, Mr. Allingham chanced to meet Ruskin at Carlyle's and brought him home to see his wife's work. She was at the time engaged on the painting of 'The Clothes-Line'. Ruskin objected to the scarlet of

❤❤

HER MAJESTY'S POST OFFICE
painted 1887

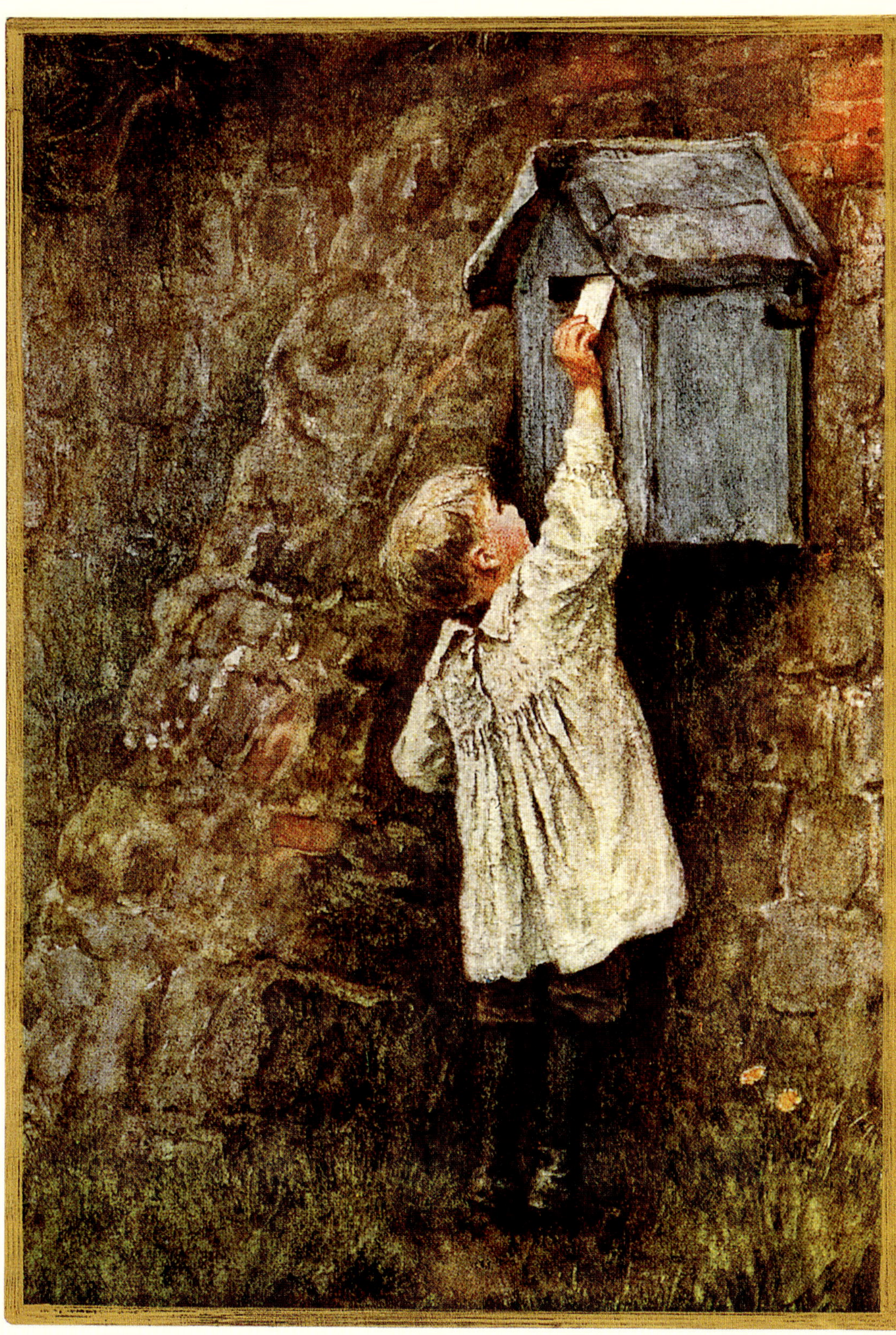

the handkerchief, and also to the woman, who he said ought to have been a rough workwoman, an opinion Mrs. Allingham did not share at the time, but which she later felt to be correct. He also saw another painting with a grey sky and asked her why she did not make her skies blue. To her reply that she thought there was often great beauty in grey skies, he growled, 'The devil sends grey skies.'

Browning, an old friend of her husband's, Mrs. Allingham sometimes saw during her residence in London. One occasion was typical of the man. He had been asked to come and see her work, which was at the time arranged at one end of a room at Trafalgar Square, Chelsea, before sending in to the Exhibition. The paintings were naturally small ones and Browning appeared to be altogether oblivious to their existence. Turning round, with his back to them, he at once commenced a story of someone who came to see an artist's work and the artist was very huffed because his visitor never took the slightest notice of his pictures, but talked to him of other subjects all the time. This, Browning considered, was no sufficient ground for his huffiness. His obliviousness to Mrs. Allingham's paintings may have been due to his having been accustomed to the pictures of his son, which were of large size, and in comparison with which Mrs. Allingham's would have been quite invisible.

Whilst Mrs. Allingham was painting Carlyle, Browning came to see him and they held a most interesting and delightful conversation on the subject of the great French writers. The alteration in Browning's demeanour from his usual bluff and breezy manner to a quiet, deferential tone during the conversation was very notable.

Of her intimacy with Tennyson, more will be said later, for she was fortunate in being able to visit him at his two homes, in Sussex and on the Isle of Wight, and illustrate them.

THE CHILDREN'S MAYPOLE
painted 1886

This scene is set in the woods at Witley.

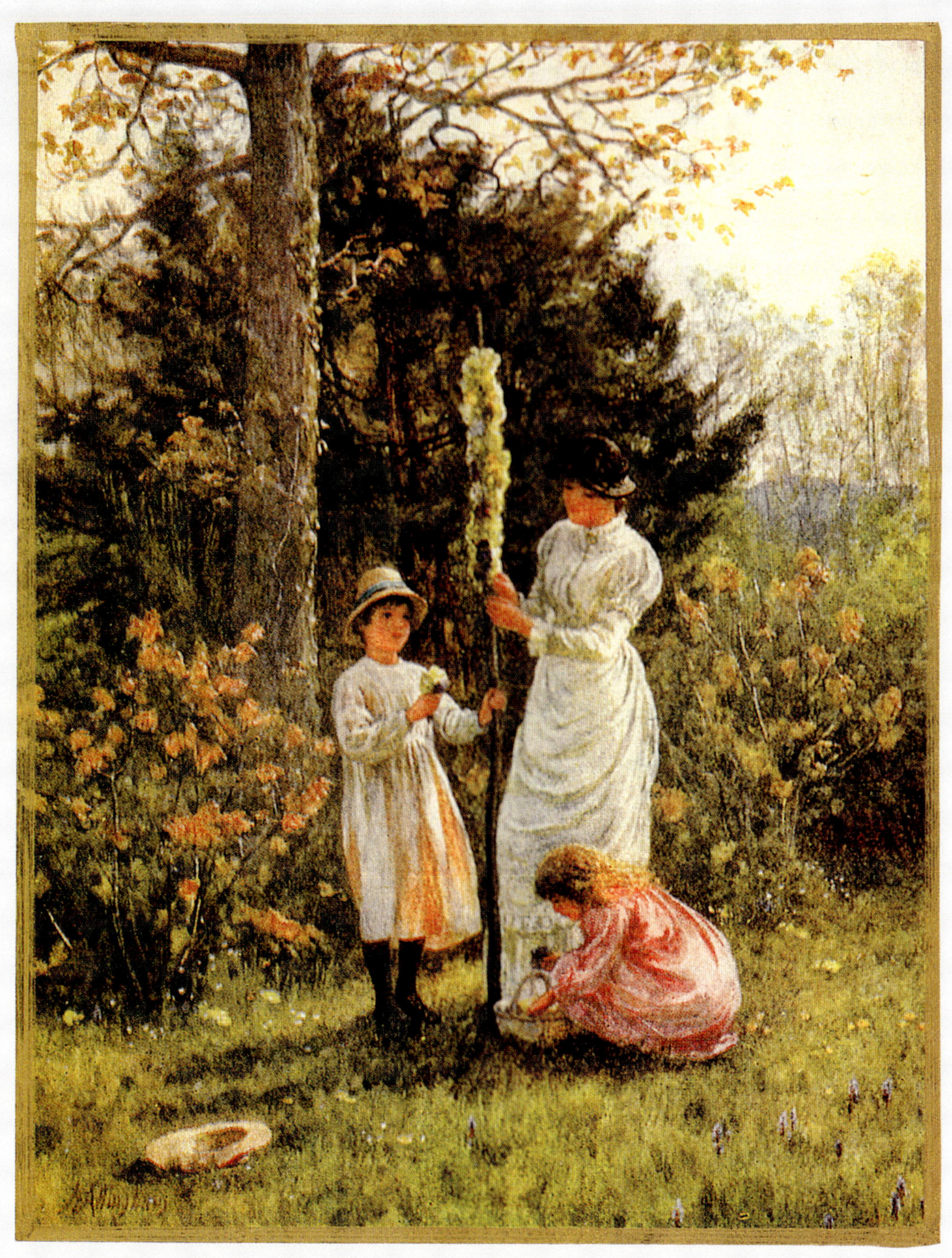

The year of her marriage was also a landmark in Mrs. Allingham's career, through the Royal Academy accepting and hanging two water-colours, both of which were sold during the Exhibition. It was, however, by another painting that she won her name.

In 1875 she was commissioned by the publisher George Bell to make a water-colour from one of the black-and-white drawings which she had done some years before for Mrs. Ewing's popular children's book *A Flat Iron for a Farthing*. The painting was seen early in 1875 by that prince of landscape water-colourists, Mr. Alfred Hunt.

The son of a successful landscape painter, Alfred Hunt had always shown a talent for drawing, although as a young man he entered Oxford University to study Classics. Like Ruskin before him, he won the Newdigate Prize for Poetry and seemed set to embark on a prosperous academic career. However, he continued to paint part-time, becoming influenced by the pre-Raphaelite principles. In 1856, at the age of twenty-six, he exhibited for the first time at the Royal Academy, where Ruskin praised his work for being 'true to Nature'. In 1864 Hunt became an Associate of the Society of Painters in Water Colours and by the time Mrs. Allingham's work attracted his notice he was at the peak of his career, recognised as one of the most original and talented painters of landscape in all England.

Mr. Hunt was an old friend of Mr. Allingham's and being told that his wife was thinking of trying for election at the Royal Society of Painters in Water Colours, kindly offered to go through her portfolios. From these he made a selection and promised to propose her at an election which was about to take place. The result fully proved the soundness of his choice, for the candidate not only secured the rare distinction of being elected on the first time of asking, but the still rarer one of securing her place in that body, so notable for its diversity of opinion when candidates were in question, with hardly a dissenting vote.

❦❦

ON THE PILGRIMS' WAY
painted 1902

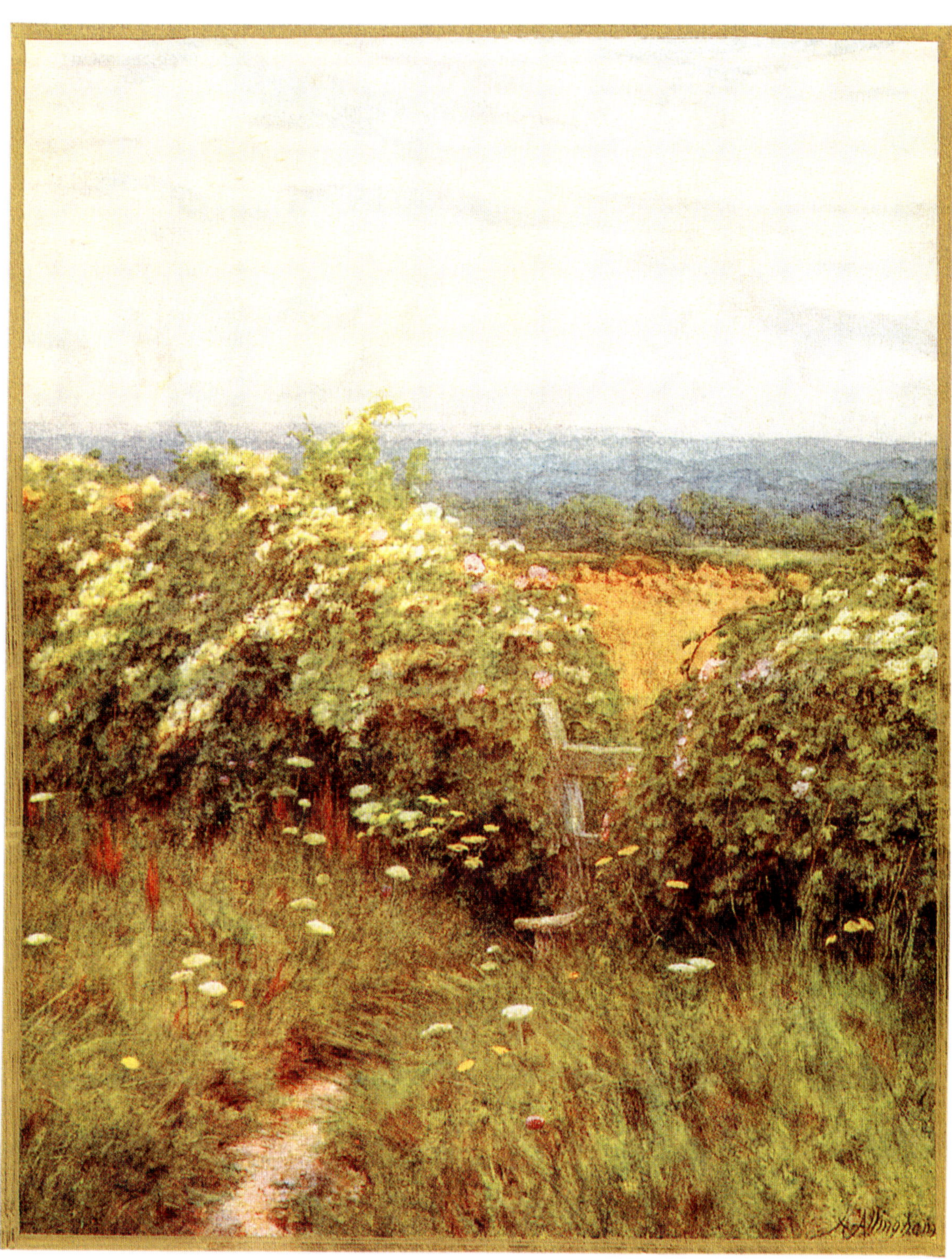

(Ladies were not admitted to the rank of full members of the Society until the year 1890, when Mrs. Allingham was, to her great pleasure and astonishment, one of the first to receive that recognition.) This election, and the fact that after her marriage she could afford to do without the monetary aid derived from black-and-white work, decided her to embark upon water-colours; although she still confined her work to figure subjects, more than one of which was be founded on her previous work in monochrome.

The last book in which her name appeared as illustrator was, appropriately enough, *Rhymes for Young Folk*, written by her husband and published by Cassell's in 1885, to which she contributed most of the illustrations. She relinquished black-and-white work without any regret, for although she was much indebted to it, it never had held her sympathies, and she always longed to express herself in colour, the medium in which she instinctively felt she had ultimately the best chance of success.

With one exception, Mrs. Allingham's work at this period was not reminiscent of the place in which she lived, the fashionable artists' quarter of Chelsea. That exception, however, disclosed to her a field in which she foresaw much delight and abundant possibilities. In the old Pensioners' Garden at Chelsea Hospital were to be found tenderly cared-for borders of humble flowers. The garden itself was a haven of repose for the old soldiers and a show-place for their visitors. Mrs. Allingham was touched by the pathos of the surroundings and thanks chiefly to the urging of her husband, she ventured on a painting of more importance than any she had hitherto attempted. It was finished in 1877 and was the first large painting she exhibited at the Society of Painters in Water Colours.

❤❤

COTTAGE AT CHIDDINGFOLD
painted 1889

This Kent cottage, pictured in early spring, displays the usual massive central chimney, but also a smaller end one, which is uncommon for a building of this size.

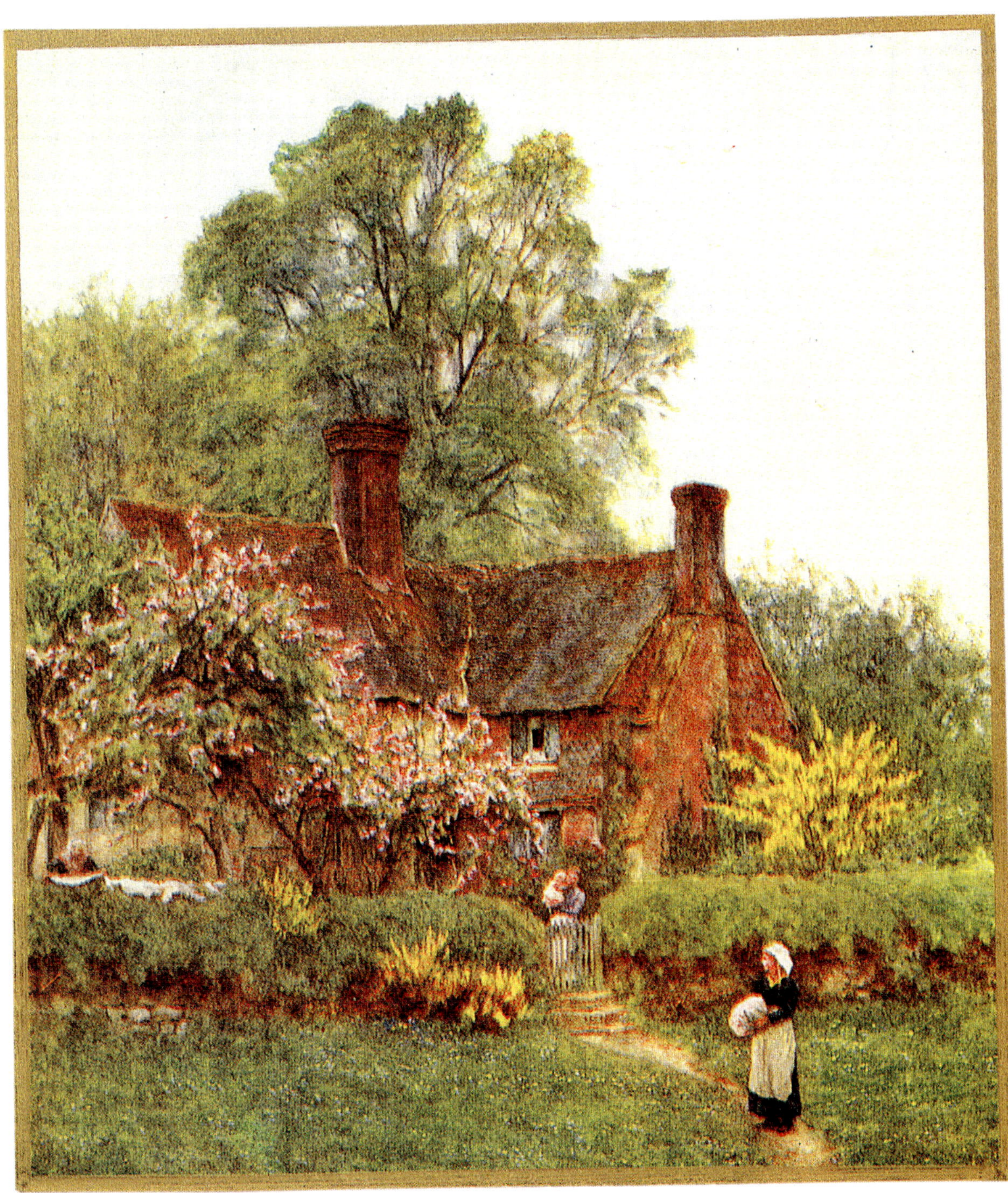

Painters – good, bad and indifferent – of the garden have for a long time been so numerous that one is apt to forget that when Mrs. Allingham first did it, painting gardens with flowers was a novelty. It is nevertheless the fact and in taking it up, especially with gardens associated with the humbler type of cottages, Mrs. Allingham was practically the originator of a new subject. So it is to the pensioners' patches at Chelsea that we are indebted for the delightful style of painting with which her name will forever be associated. The Chelsea Hospital aroused in her a desire to attack gardens possessing greater possibilities than a town-stunted patch, although this desire was not gratified until two years later when, during a visit to Shere in Surrey in the spring of 1879, she painted the first of many cottages and flowers from Nature.

In 1881, after the death of Carlyle, Chelsea had attractions for neither husband nor wife, and with a young family growing up and calling for larger and healthier quarters, they gave up the house in Trafalgar Square for one at Witley in Surrey, a hamlet close to Haslemere, which Mrs. Allingham had visited the year before, and in the midst of countryside which her friend and mentor Myles Birket Foster had already done much to popularise, having resided at a beautiful house there for many years.

IN WORMLEY WOOD
painted 1886

In a description of this picture written in 1903, the author laments the disappearance of thatch as a covering for old cottages. This dwelling, when it was painted, was one of the few remaining examples in the area and it probably escaped 'modernisation' because of its isolated position amidst the woods, on the outskirts of Witley in Surrey.

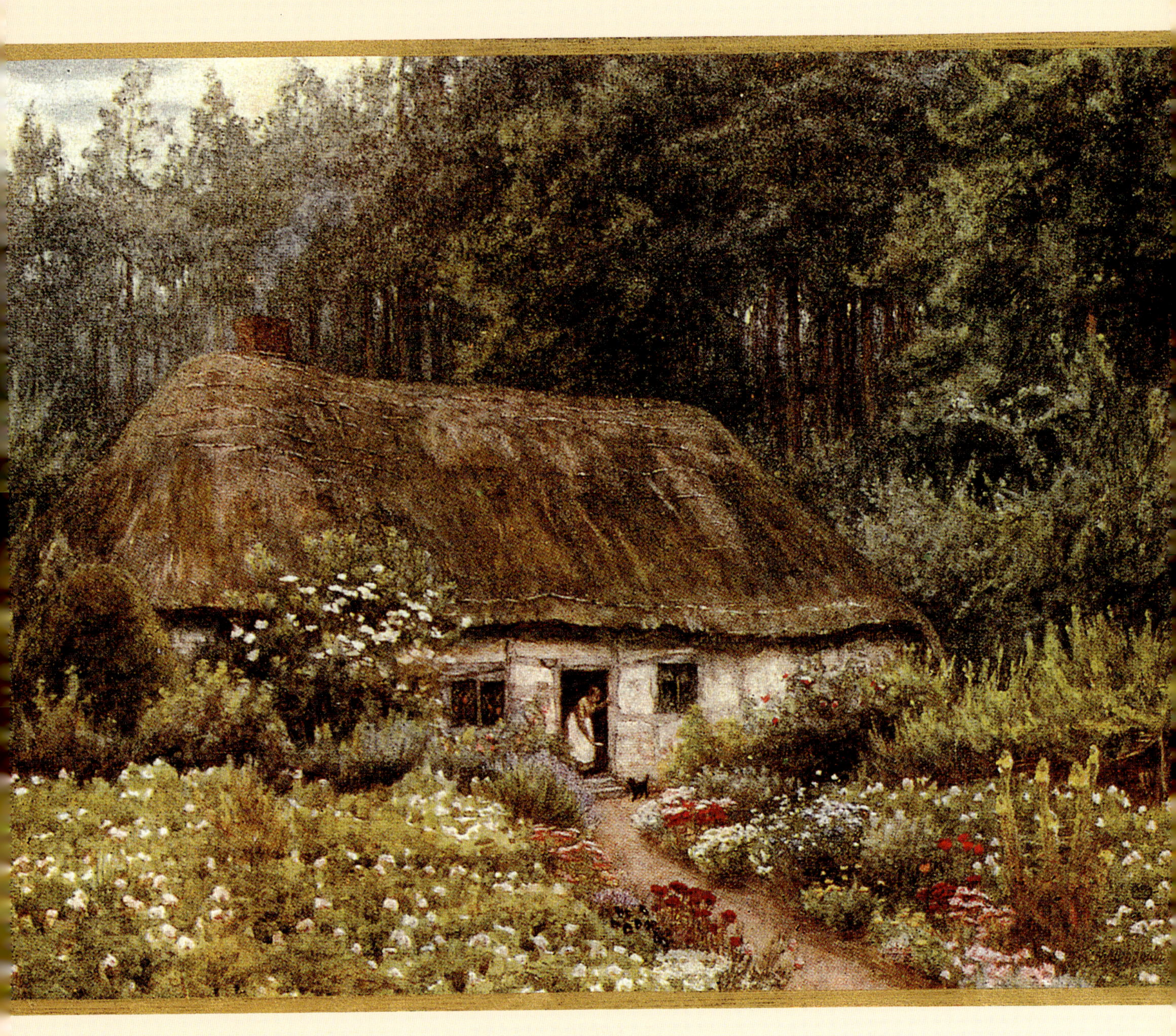

THE MOVE TO SURREY

There are few fairer counties in England than Surrey, and of Surrey the fairest portion is by common consent the extreme south-western edge which skirts Sussex to the south and Hampshire to the west. Travellers from London to Portsmouth by the London and South-Western Railway on leaving Guildford pass through the middle of the right angle which this corner makes, and cut the corner two miles beyond Haslemere almost exactly at the point where the three counties meet. As the steep rise of nearly 300 feet which has to be surmounted in the six miles which divide Witley from Haslemere is being negotiated by the train, the most unobservant passenger must be struck by the singularly beautiful wooded character of the country on either side, and by the far-extended view which is unfolded as the eye looks southward over the Weald of Sussex.

So wrote Marcus Huish, describing the area that was to be Mrs. Allingham's home for most of the 1880s.

It was to Sandhills, near Witley, that Mrs. Allingham went to live in 1881 with her growing family. In this corner of Surrey she found ample material for almost all her work during the next few years; and it was there that she returned at intervals for the majority of those cottage subjects which the public called for from the moment of her first portrayal of them .

Sandhills lay on the Haslemere side of Witley, on a sloping common of heather and gorse, topped with fir trees. It was a healthy and bracing spot, and one calculated to induce a painter to energetic work, and a delight in

❦❦

THE STILE
painted 1883

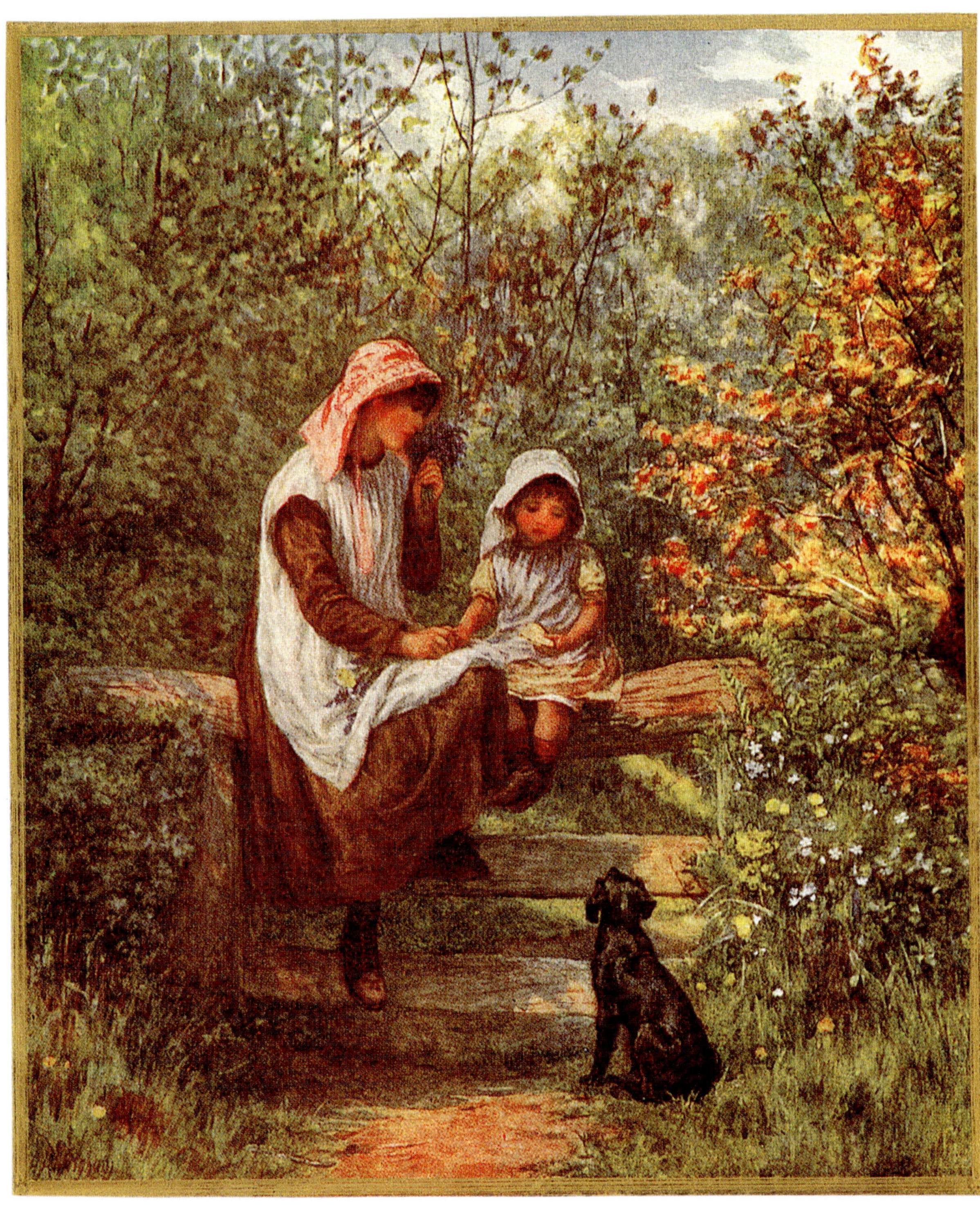

doing it. Subjects lay close at hand, the Sandhills garden furnishing many of them. In the spring the country round was decked with primroses, bluebells and cowslips in the woods, hedgerows and fields; and it was indeed pleasurable to ramble from copse to field and back again.

It will be readily understood that such a beneficial change in her surroundings as that from Trafalgar Square, Chelsea, to Sandhills, Witley, had a strong and positive effect upon Mrs. Allingham's Art. Hitherto her work had, by the exigencies of fortune, concentrated almost entirely on the figure. It was studio work, done for the most part under pressure of time; she rarely had any say in the selection of subject, which was therefore often altogether unsympathetic. Finding herself now in the presence of Nature of a kind that appealed to her and which she could appreciate untrammelled by any conditions, it is not surprising that – unwittingly, no doubt, at first – she began to prefer that side of Art which presented itself under so much more favourable conditions.

She had first tasted the delight of painting *en plein air* at Shere during a spring and summer a few years earlier and she had been passionately happy watching the changes and developments of the seasons, being in the fields, lanes and copses all day and every day. Almost as full a feast had followed at Haslemere in 1880. When these were succeeded by a permanent residence in front of Nature, studio work become more and more trying and unsatisfactory.

To most people of an artistic temperament the abandonment of the figure for landscape would never have been the subject of a moment's consideration, for it would have appeared to them the desertion of a higher for a lower grade of Art. But from the time of her arrival in the country there seems never to have been any doubt in Mrs. Allingham's mind as to the direction which her Art should take. The pleasure of

A Cottage at Hambledon
painted 1886

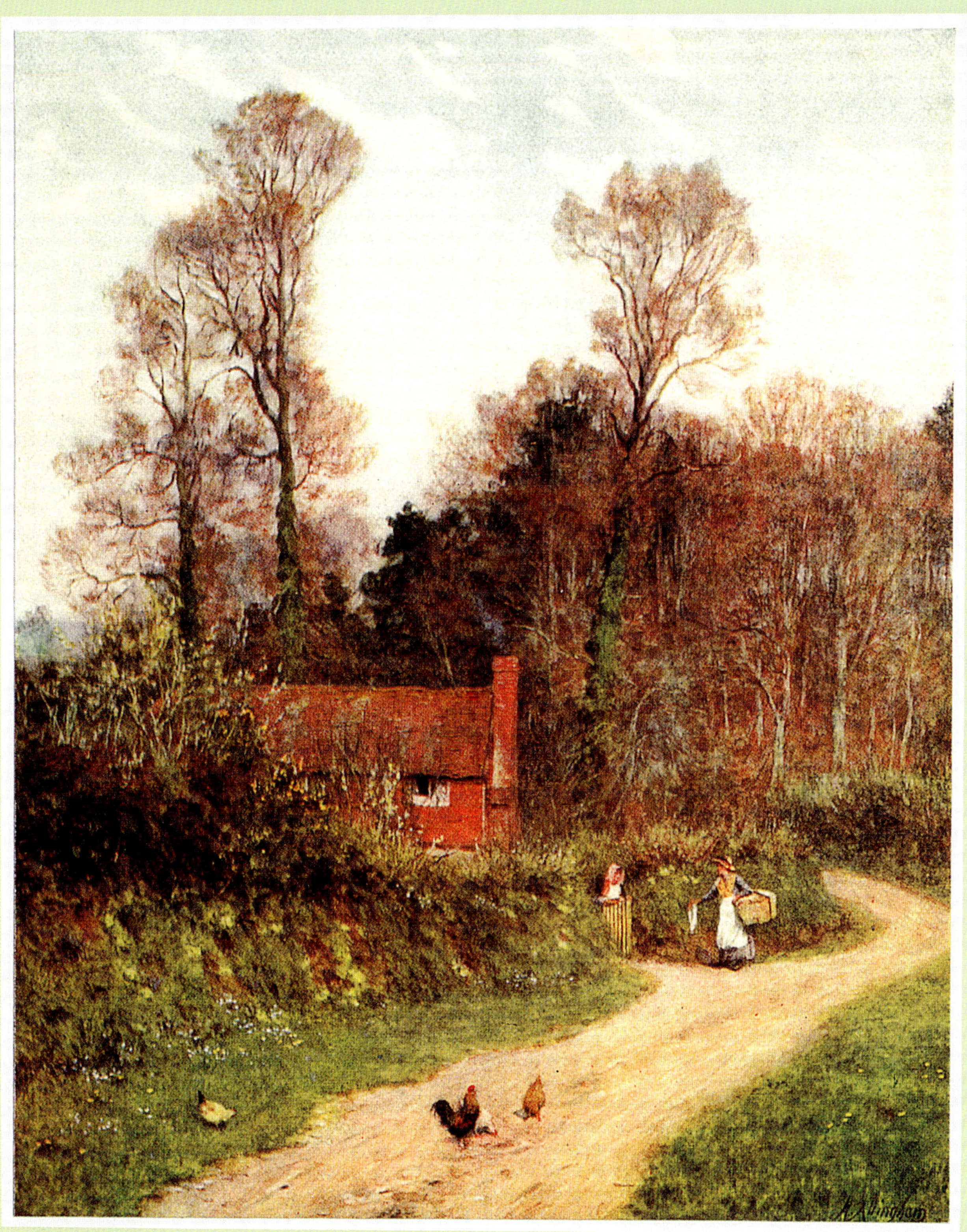

sitting down in the open air before Nature, whose aspects and moods she could select at her own will and at her own time, was infinitely preferable to the toil and trouble of illustrating the ideas of others, or building up scenes, often improbable ones, of her own creation.

From this time onwards, then, we find her drifting away from the figure, but not altogether, or at once, for as her family grew up, she enjoyed placing on record aspects of her home life: scenes of infant life in the nursery, such as 'Pat-a-Cake' and 'The Children's Tea'; in the schoolroom, such as 'Lessons'; and out of school hours, such as 'Bubbles' and 'The Children's Maypole'. In one and all of these her own family are the chief actors.

Seeing these pictures encouraged friends and others to press upon her commissions for portraits of their own children; but this branch of work promptly drew down upon her the disapproval of Ruskin, who wrote: 'I am indeed sorrowfully compelled to express my regret that she should have spent unavailing pains in finishing single heads, which are at the best uninteresting miniatures, instead of fulfilling her true gift and doing what the Lord made her for in representing the gesture, character and humour of charming children in country landscapes.'

This change naturally did not come over her work all at once. Her presentations of the countryside began in earnest shortly after she settled at Witley; but the figure as the dominant feature continued for another six years; in fact, for the whole of her time at Witley we find it now and again, and do not part with it as such until 1890. After that, she produced hardly a single example, giving as her reason for the change that she came to the conclusion that she could put as much interest into a figure two or three inches high as into one three times as large, and that she could paint it better; for in painting large figures out of doors there was always a difficulty in making them look anything else than they were, namely 'posing models'.

❤❤

IN A WITLEY LANE
painted 1887

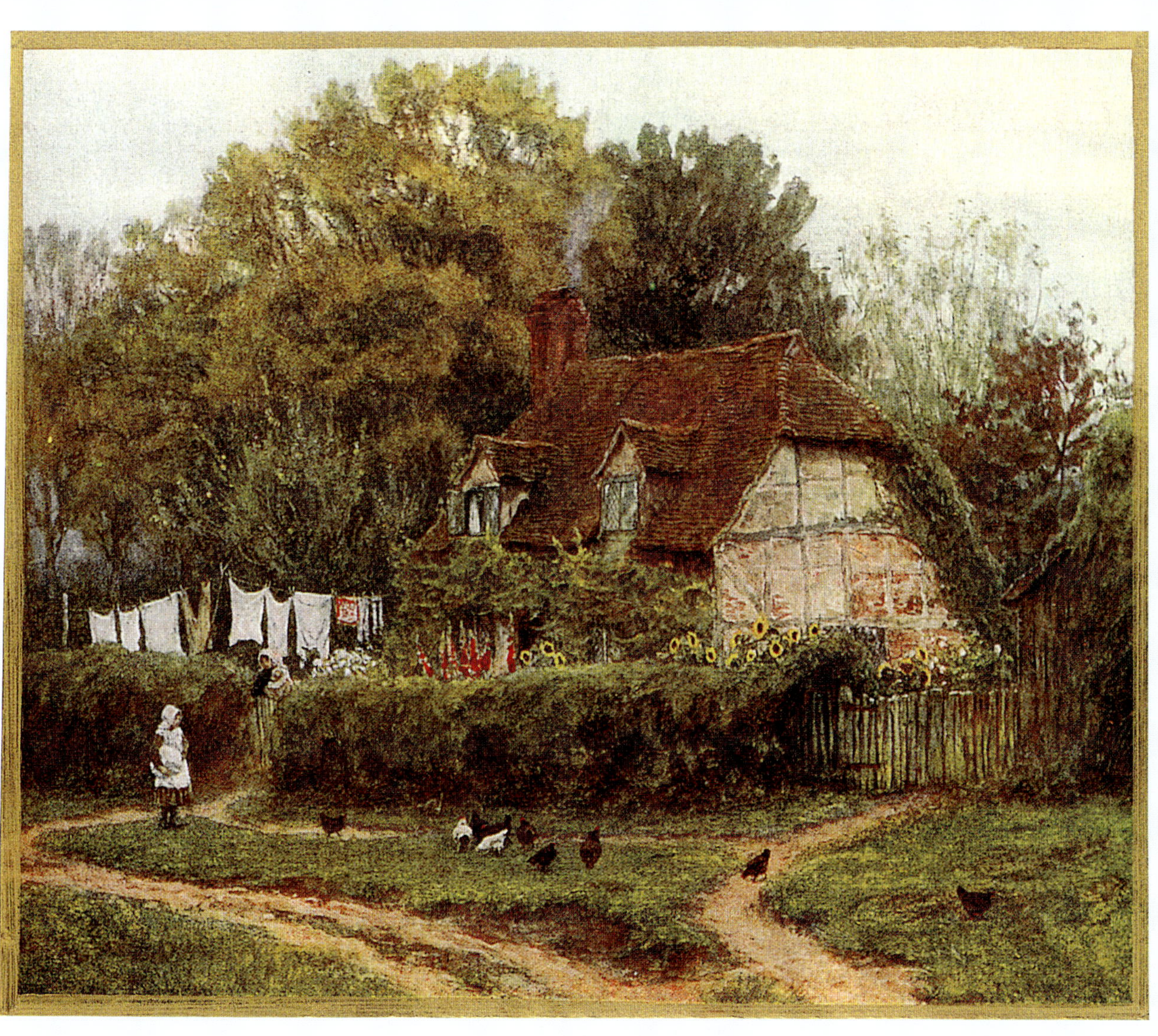

But if the figure ceased to occupy the foremost position, it was still there, and was always present to add a charming vitality to all that she did. To people a landscape with figures, of captivating mien, each taking its proper position and each adding to the interest of the whole, is a gift possessed by few landscapists. Mrs. Allingham frequently garnered for future use a mass of valuable material, so that she was never at a loss for the right adjunct to fit the right place.

Her doing so was, in the first instance, due entirely to her husband. He said, truly, that the introduction of animals and birds, in fact any form of life, gave scale and interest to a picture, and from the first he urged her to begin making studies. There is not the slightest doubt that she owed very much to him that habit of thinking out appropriate figures, as she always tried, and with exceptional success, to be accessories to every landscape.

Her sketch-books, consequently, are full not only of men, women and children and their immediate belongings, but of most of the animal life which follows in their train. I say 'most' because she had preferences. Horses, cattle and sheep she featured few of, only occasionally introducing them in distant hay or harvest fields. Nor had she much interest in dogs, but for cats she had a great fondness and they animate a large number of her scenes. Fowls, pigeons and the like she painted to the life and she appears to have been thoroughly acquainted with their habits; but other winged creatures, save an occasional robin, she avoided. Rabbits, wild and tame, she often introduced.

AN OLD HOUSE AT WEST TARRING

painted 1900

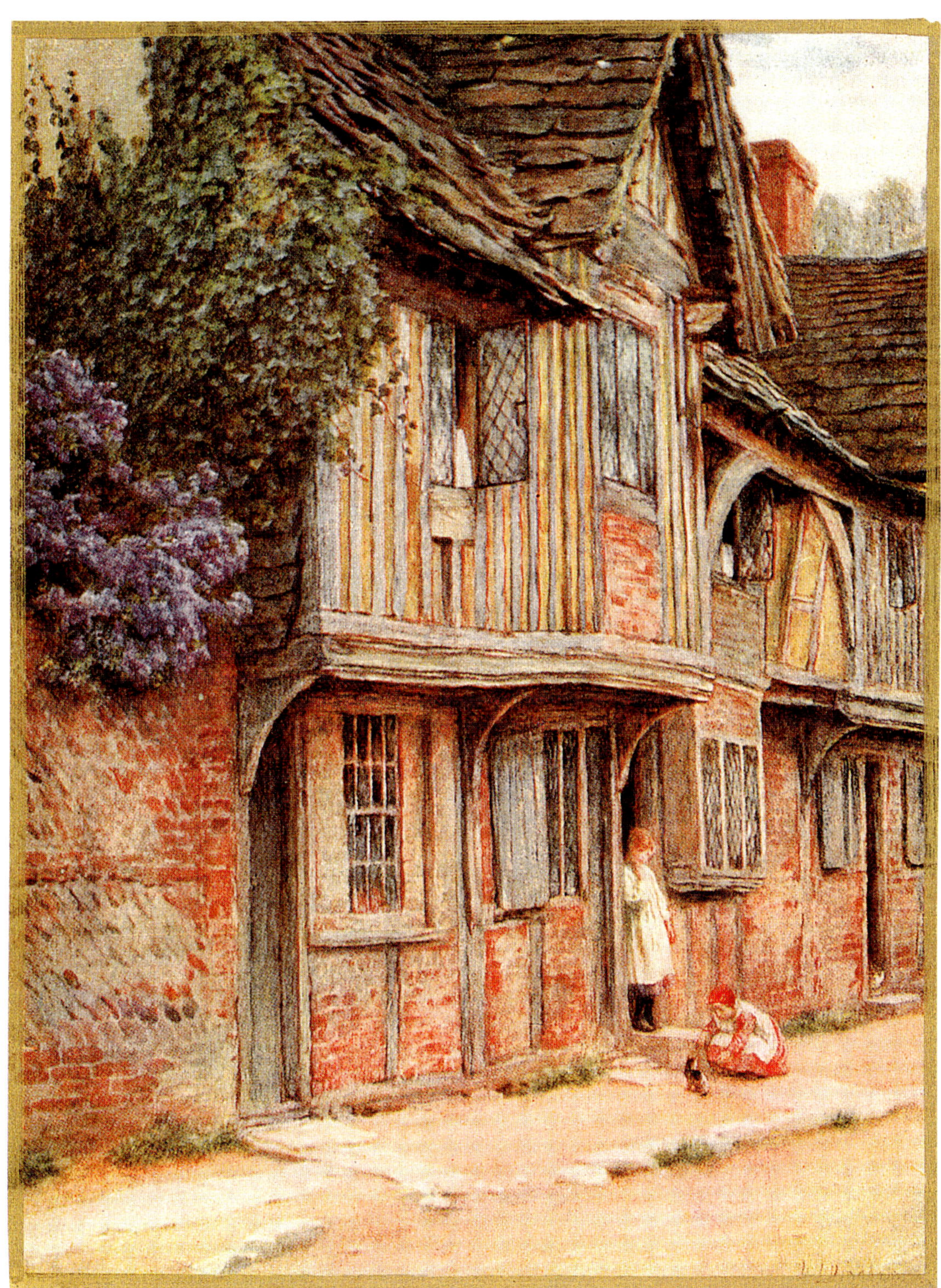

PAINTING IN THE COUNTRYSIDE

When Mrs. Allingham finally cut herself away from figure painting – or, perhaps more accurately, drifted away from it because of the influence of her surroundings – she did not, as so many do, devote herself to a single style of landscape art. Her journeyings in search of subjects were for some years neither many nor extensive, for a woman painter with a family growing up around her did not at that time have the same opportunities as a man. Hence the ground she covered was almost entirely confined to the 'Home Counties', with an occasional diversion to the Isle of Wight, Dorset, Gloucestershire and Cheshire. Surrey and Kent furnished most of her material, the former naturally being drawn upon most often during her life at Witley and the latter after she returned to live in London in 1888.

This inability to roam anywhere she chose was doubtless helpful in compelling her to vary her subjects, for she had of necessity to paint whatever came within her reach. But her energy also contributed its share, for it enabled her to search the whole countryside wherever she was, and gather in a dozen suitable scenes where another might only discover one.

As evidence of this we may give the case of a corner of Kent where she went again and again, and where she was always able to find ample material to her liking. In the mile that separated the station from the farmhouse where she encamped lay a cottage that she painted from every side, a brick kiln that she had her eye on, an old yew and a clump of elms. Arriving at the farm-gate she could point to the modest floral display in front that sufficed for 'In

❤❤

DRYING CLOTHES
painted 1886

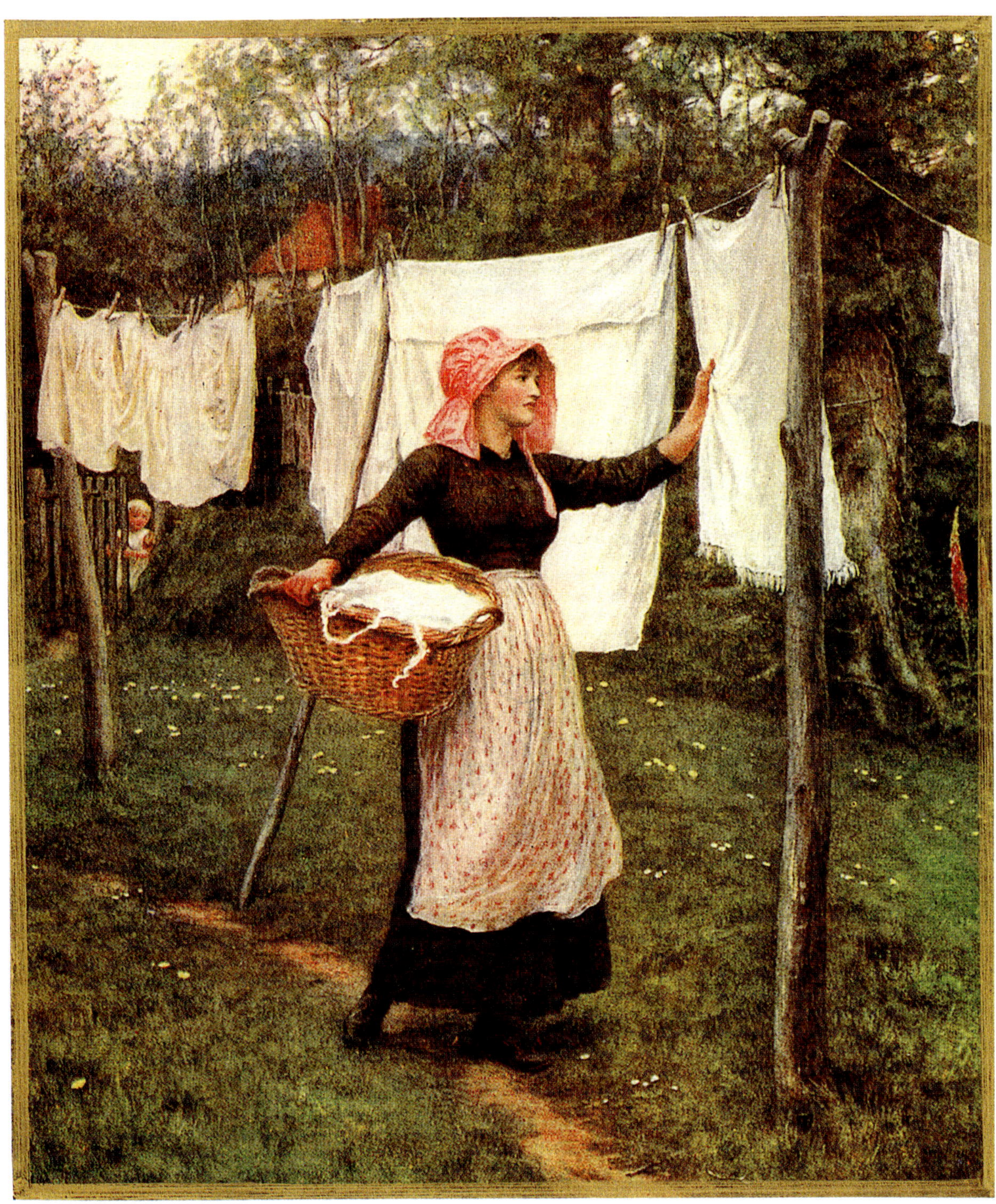

the Farmhouse Garden', whilst over the way were the buildings of 'A Kentish Farmyard'. Entering the house the visitor may not be much impressed by the view from her sitting-room window, but under the artist's hands it became a silvern sheet of daisies. 'On the Pilgrim's Way" is a field or so away, whilst a short walk up the downs behind the house finds us in the presence of the originals of 'Spring on the Kentish Downs' and 'The Old Yew Tree'. A drive across the vale brought her to Crockham Hill and Ide Hill, both the subject of paintings in this book.

This description of the variety of the artist's work within a single small area will show that it is difficult to divide it into distinct categories. It is perhaps easiest to separate this phase of her output into the following divisions: woods, lanes and fields; cottages; and gardens. We shall therefore consider these in this and the following chapters, dealing here with the first of them.

Midway through her life at Witley, the Fine Art Society induced Mrs. Allingham to undertake, as the subject for an Exhibition, the portrayal of the countryside under its four seasonal aspects of spring, summer, autumn and winter. She completed her task, and the result was shown in 1886 in an Exhibition, but a glance at the catalogue shows in which direction her preference lay; for whilst spring and summer between them accounted for more than fifty pictures, only seven answered for autumn and six, of which half were interiors, illustrated winter. These proportions may not perhaps have represented the ratio of her affections, but of her physical ability to portray each of the seasons. Autumn leaves and tints no doubt appealed to her artistic eye as much as spring or summer hues, but for some reason, perhaps that of health, illustrations were few and far between of the time of year

❦❦

COTTAGE AT SHOTTERHILL, NEAR HASLEMERE
painted 1891

This cottage was situated exactly at the junction of three counties: Surrey, Sussex and Hampshire. It is unusually large and well protected from the elements by its low-lying tile roof.

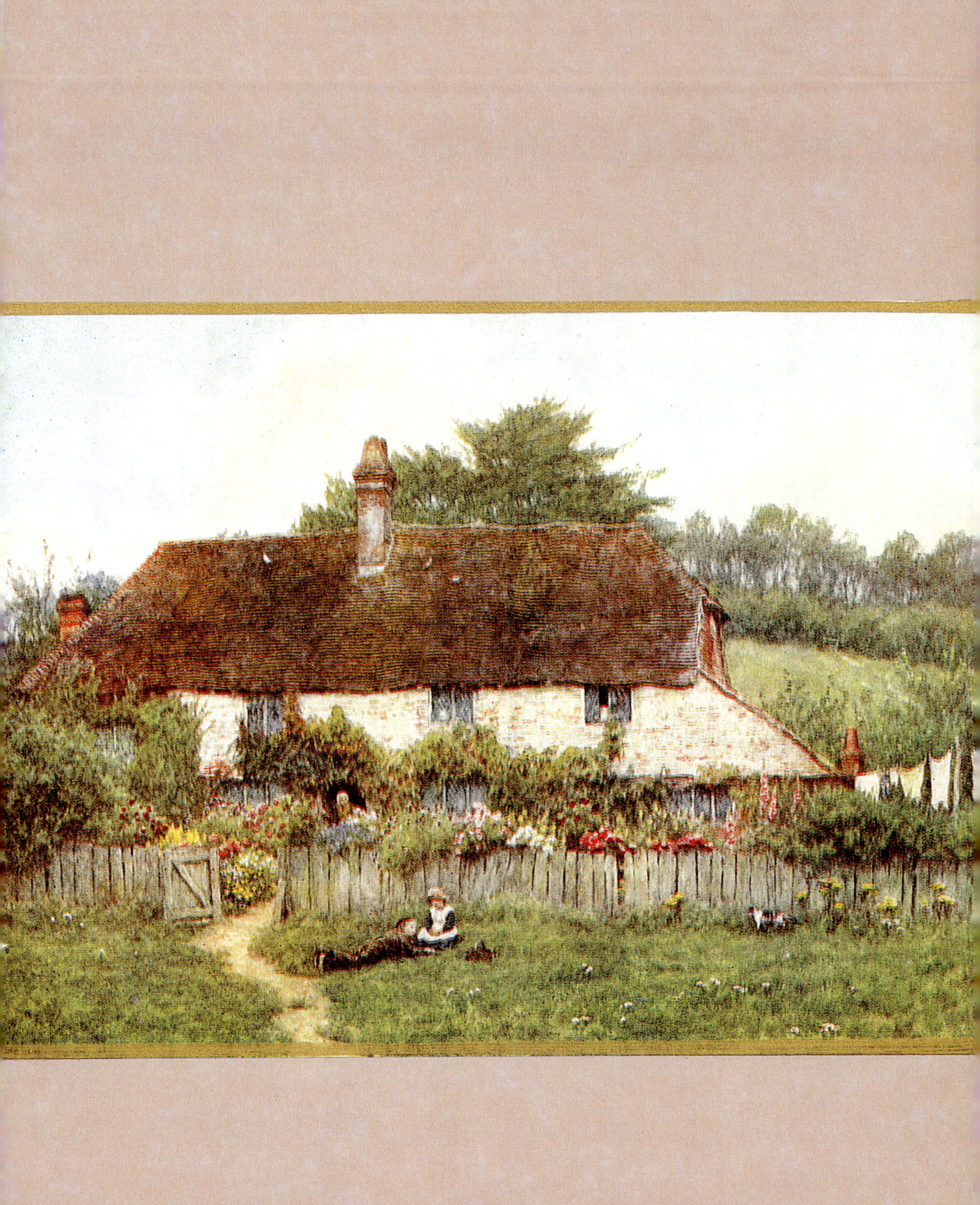

When yellow leaves, or none, or few, do hang
Upon those boughs which shake against the cold,
Bare ruin'd choirs, where late the sweet birds sang.

In so selecting she differed from Mr. Ruskin, who decreed that 'a tree is never meant to be drawn with all its leaves on, any more than a day when its sun is at noon. One draws the day in its morning or eventide, the tree in its spring or autumn dress.'

This naturally exaggerated dictum was the opposite of Mrs. Allingham's practice. She almost invariably waited until the trees had completely donned their spring garb, and left them ere they doffed their summer dress. She was not averse, however, to venturing forth as soon as the first signs of spring should emerge from their winter slumbering. The scene of 'Spring on the Kentish Downs' (opposite) is of very early spring. The highest trees show no sign of it save at their outermost edges. Hazels alone, and they only in the shelter, have shed their flowery tassels and assumed a leafage which is still immature in colour. The sprawling trails of the traveller's joy, which rioted over everything the previous autumn, are still without any trace of returning vitality.

In 'Spring in the Oakwood', on the other hand, the season is more advanced and the painting shows one of the rare occasions on which Mrs. Allingham utilised sunlight and shadow. It also proves that, however rarely she chose to use this approach, it was from no lack of ability, for it is now introduced

❧ ❧

SPRING ON THE KENTISH DOWNS

painted 1900

Out of the city, far away
With spring to-day!
Where copses tufted with primrose
Give one repose.
William Allingham

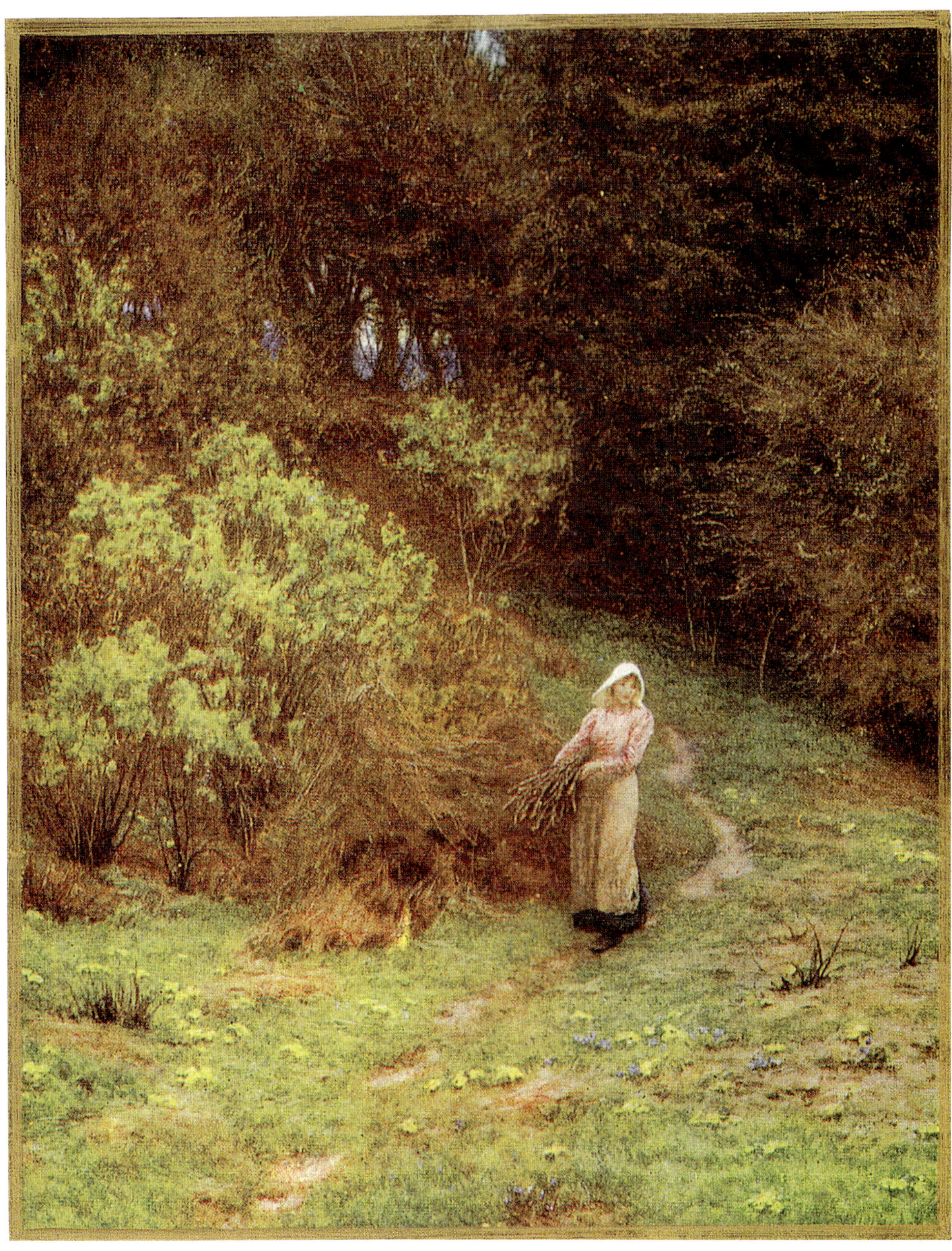

with a difficult effect, namely, blue flowers under a low raking light. The artist's eye was doubtless attracted by the unusual visitation of a bright warm sun on a spring day, and determined to perpetuate it. The juxtaposition of the two primaries, blue and yellow, is always a happy one in Nature, but especially with such a mass of sapphire blue.

SPRING IN THE OAKWOOD
painted 1903

The wood pictured here lay on the Kentish Downs, where strong winds are always a feature, as shown by the contorted boughs.

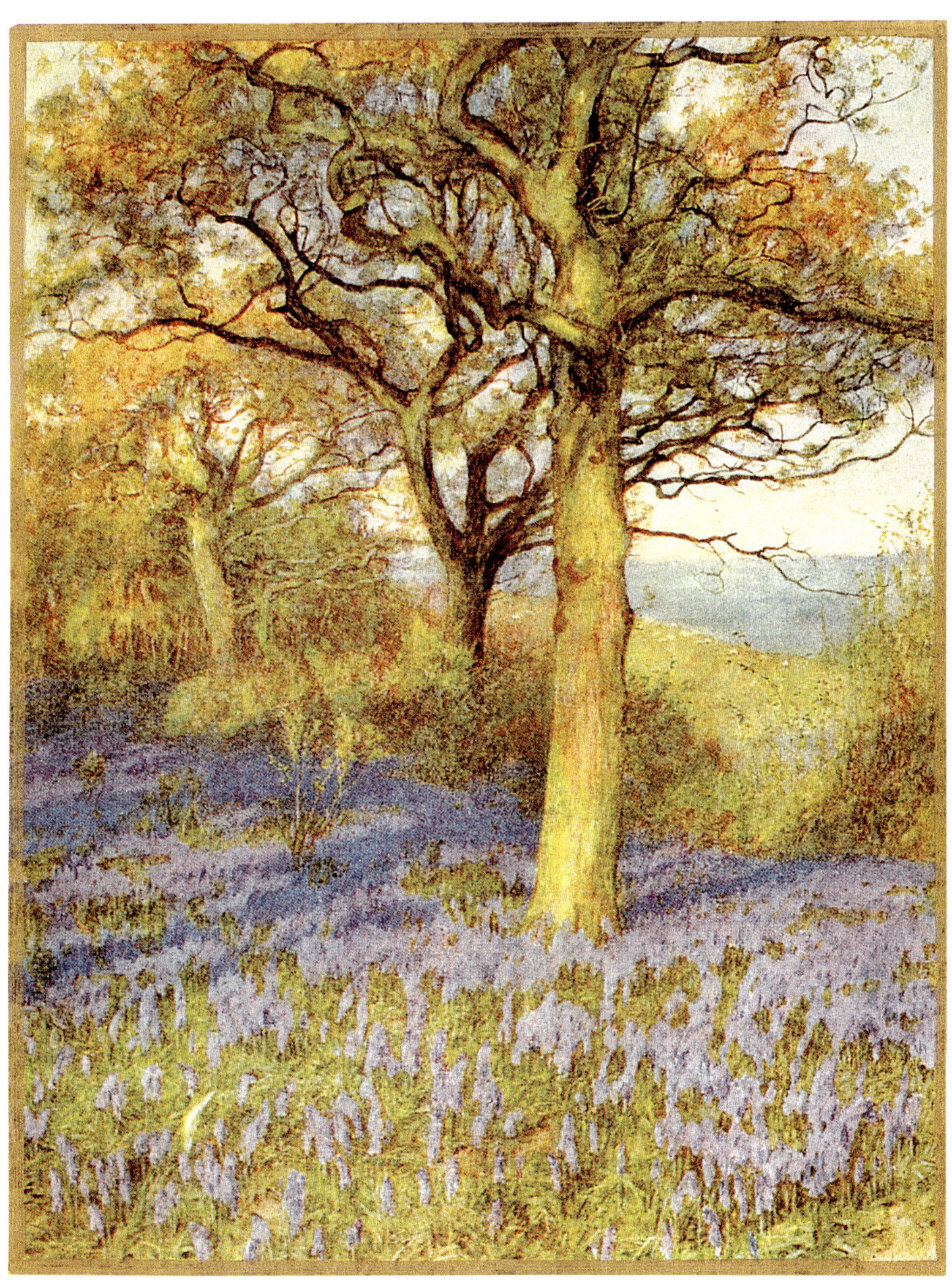

THE COTTAGE PAINTINGS

'Mrs. Allingham's cottages' have for a long time been a household word amongst connoisseurs of English water-colours, and no collection is deemed complete without one. For their value does not consist solely in their beauty as works of Art, but in their recording in line and colour a most interesting, but unfortunately vanishing phase of English domestic architecture. They are, in fact, veritable portraits; for the artist, whilst naturally selecting those best suited to her purpose, prided herself on presenting them with an accuracy of structural feature which is not always the case in works of this kind, where the painter considers that he can improve his picture by an addition here and an omission there.

So many of Mrs. Allingham's cottages have been taken from the counties of Surrey and Sussex, that it may be of interest to give some short description of their distinguishing features. One is apt to pass them by, whether in reality or in their portraits, without a thought as to their structure, or an idea that they have evolved along very marked lines from primitive types, influenced in almost every instance by local surroundings. The information in this chapter is drawn from the writings of a contemporary architect.

In the early days of housebuilding the use of local materials was naturally a distinctive feature of poorer dwellings, to an even greater extent than in the case of the houses of the well-to-do, and in like manner the architecture of the better built houses influenced the more humble ones. Change in the early days was seldom indulged in, and a style which had been found to be convenient was persevered with for generation after generation, individuality and suitability to site making each building distinct from its neighbour.

❤ ❤

A CHESHIRE COTTAGE, ALDERLEY EDGE

painted 1898

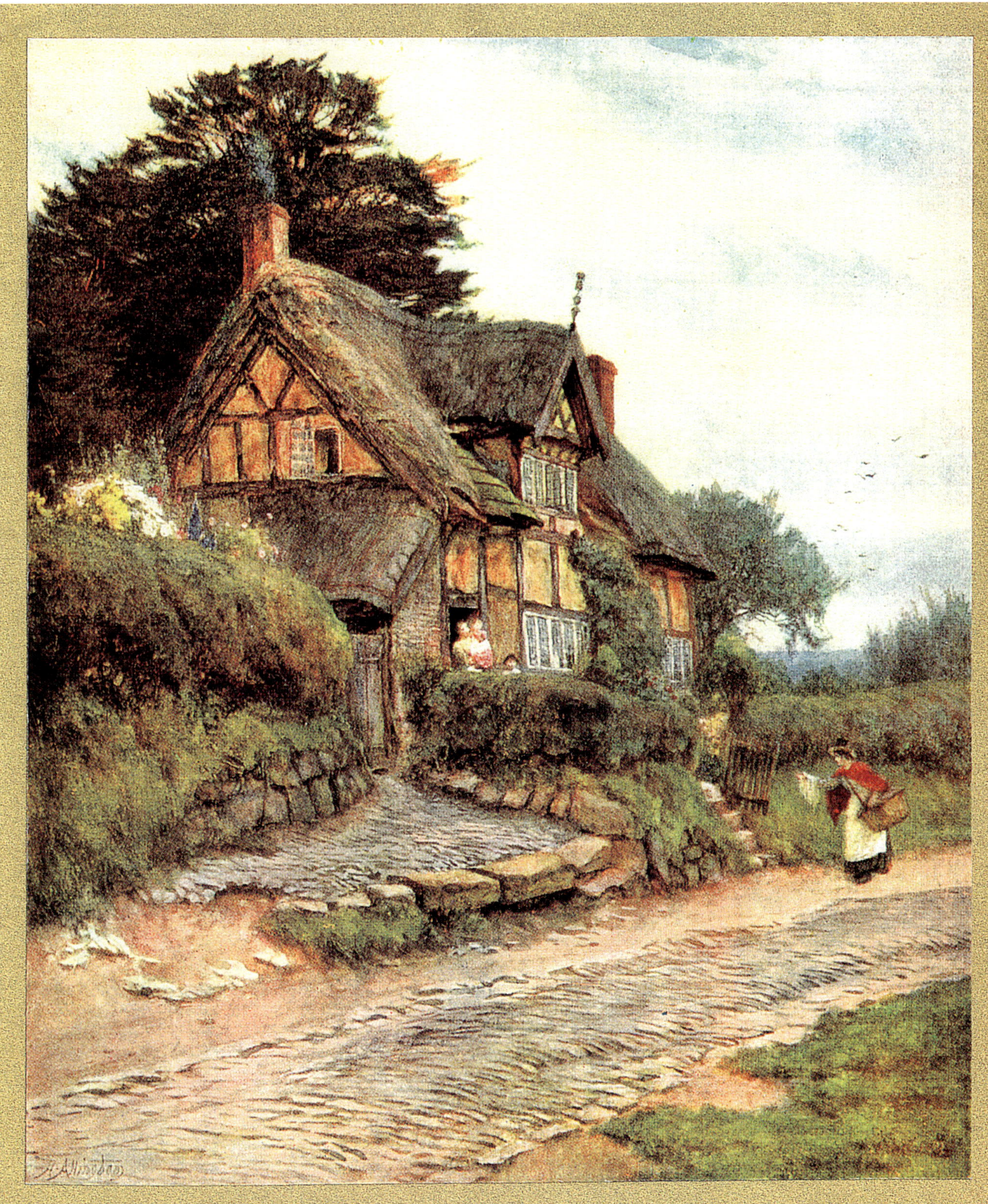

For instance, a prevailing type throughout England of an early English country house consisted of an oblong hall in the centre, with the offices and other rooms at either end forming wings, the ground plan thus taking the shape of a letter E or H. The same plan may still be discerned in the yeomen's dwellings, although it is less easily traceable because in later times the central common room was divided up into compartments. Types of this kind may, however, be found in almost every village in the south-eastern counties, and an example will be seen in 'The Six Bells' and the house at West Tarring, near Worthing, where the central portion falls back from the gable ends. This arrangement of a central hall used as a living room, which had been out of favour for some centuries, was curiously enough coming back into fashion at the time when Mrs. Allingham was painting so many of these cottages.

Local materials, as we have said, having much to do with the structure, the type of dwelling that we may expect to find in counties where wood was plentiful, and the cost of preparing and putting it on the ground less than that of quarrying, shaping, and carrying stone, is the picturesque, timber-formed cottage.

The construction is simple in the extreme. A plan was set out and a base or foundation wall built, usually of brick or stone, high enough to keep the sill well above the ground. Into this sill heavy posts of timber, some eight or nine inches square, were fixed upright, about seven or eight feet apart, those at the corners being generally larger and formed of the butt of a tree placed root upwards, with the top part curving diagonally outwards, to carry the angle-posts of the upper storey. Upon these main posts beams were laid across the building, projecting forward some eighteen inches in front of the framing below, and showing in the rooms below. Into the beams others were connected longitudinally, and to these latter again the floor joists were tenoned, projecting the same distance as the main beams. In houses of the sixteenth century the ends of the joists were covered (as in the house at West

❦❦

THE FISH-SHOP, HASLEMERE
painted 1887

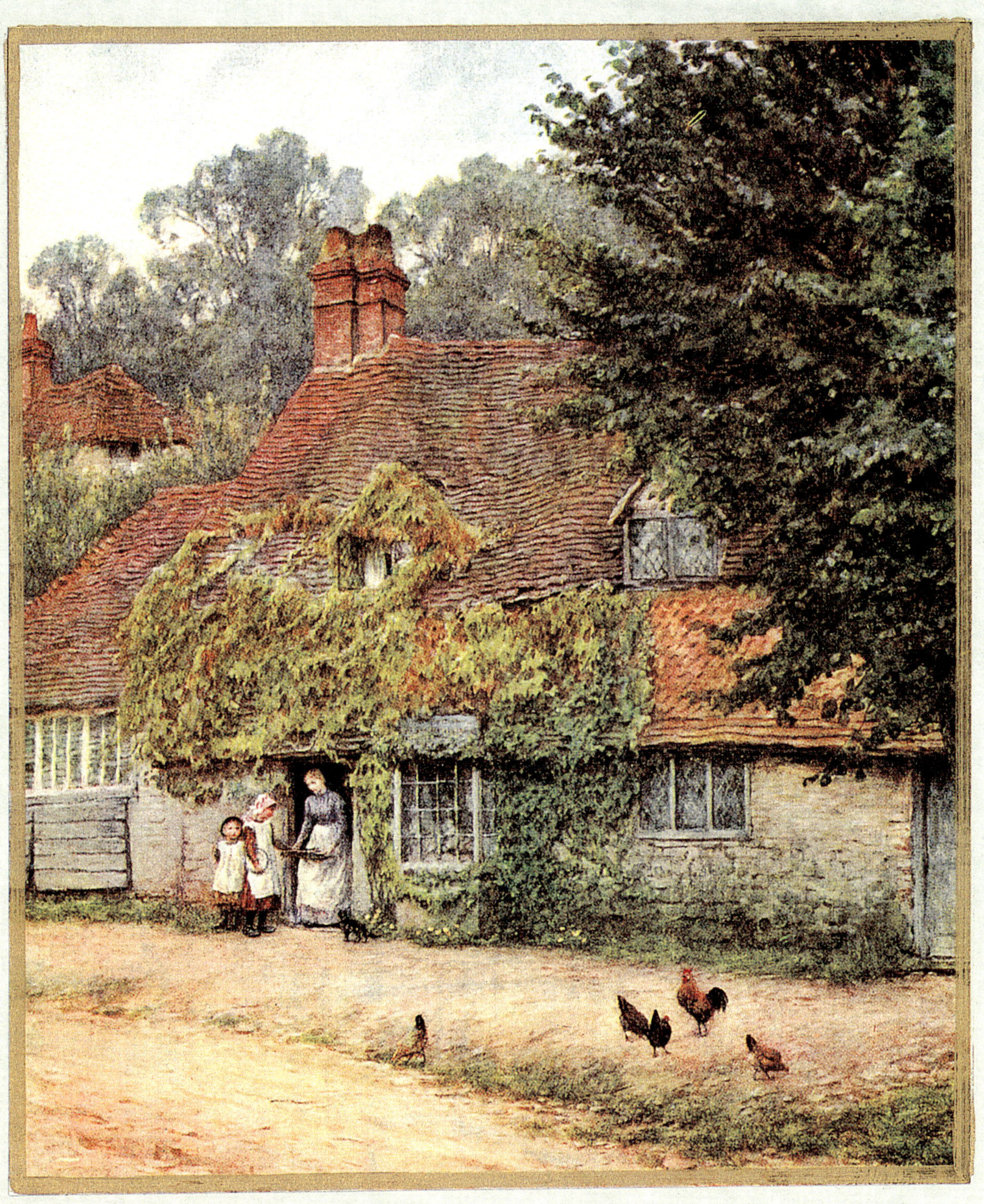

Tarring) with a large and deeply moulded fascia, but in later examples such as 'The Six Bells' this was abandoned and the ends of the joists were merely rounded off. The framing of the upper storey then followed that of the ground floor, the sill being now laid on the ends of the overhanging timbers.

The roof-tree was always of hand-hewn oak, and it was this, according to Birket Foster, which gave to many of the old roofs their pleasant curves away from the central chimney. The ordinary unseasoned sawn deal of the modern roof may sway in any direction.

The spaces between the main uprights were filled in with windows or framing. The timbers of the framing were generally about eight inches apart and nearly as much in width, the closeness of the timbering seen in the West Tarring front showing that it is early work. In the better-to-do houses, such as this, the divisions between the timbers were filled with bricks, but in others wattles or laths and chopped straw and clay were used, and the surface was then plastered flush with the woodwork.

Most of these frameworks were built of oak, which generally shrinks. When this happened the joints came apart and decayed, and it was necessary, in order to keep out the weather, either to plaster them all over, cover them with deal boarding, or, where they were procurable, with tiles, as in 'Valewood

❤❤

THE BASKET WOMAN
painted 1887

The then art critic of The Times *singled out this picture as 'taking rank amongst the very best of Mrs. Allingham's work, and the very model of what an English water-colour should be, with its woodside cottage, its tangled hedges, its background of sombre fir trees, and figures of the girl with basket, and of the cottages to whom she is offering her wares, showing as it does intense love for our beautiful south country landscape, with the power of seizing its most picturesque aspects with truth of eye and delicacy of hand.'*

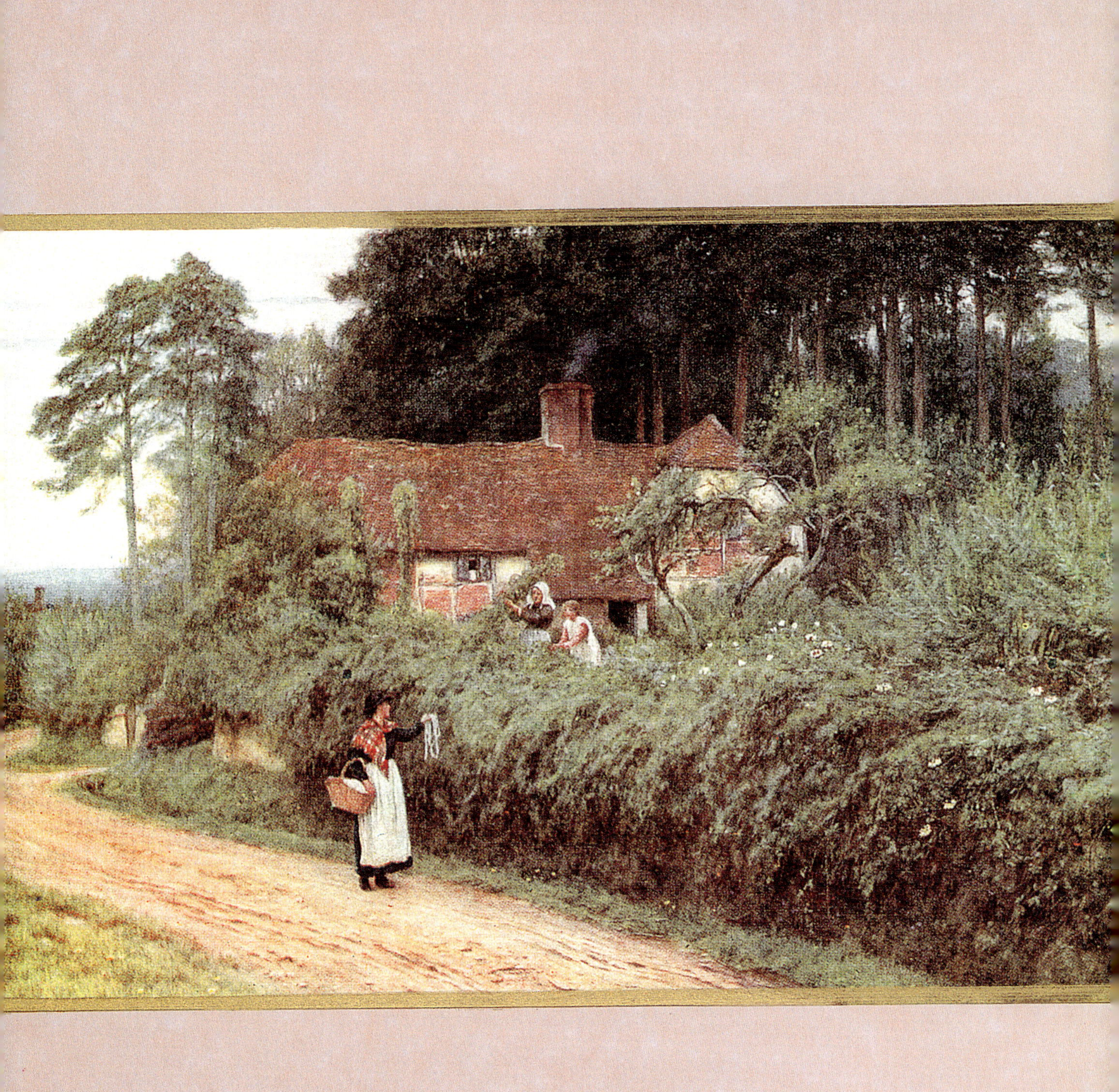

Farm' and 'The Cottage at Shottermill'. In Kent and Sussex these are constantly met with in some part or another of the building, perhaps only in a gable end, most often in the upper storey, sometimes over the whole building, but of course, principally, where it was most exposed to the weather, as at Shottermill and 'The Cottage at Chiddingfold'. The tiles used were generally flatter and thinner than those on the roof, and when bedded in mortar they made a thoroughly weather-proof wall.

In the older houses the rooms were low and the roof was carried down well over the side walls, so that the upper storey was usually badly lighted and worse ventilated. Little use was made of the large space in the roof, but this omission adds much to the picturesqueness of the exterior, for the roofs gain in simplicity by their unbroken surface and treatment. It is somewhat surprising that the old builders did not recognise this costly disregard of space.

The roofs, like the framework, testified to the geological formation and agricultural conditions of the district. In those where the land was chiefly arable, or the distance from market considerable, wheaten thatch was the usual and most comfortable covering, for it is warm in winter and cool in summer, just the reverse of the tiles or slates which have practically supplanted it. In other districts the cottages were covered with what were known as stone slates, thick and heavy. Roofs to carry the weight of these had always to be flattened, with the result that they required mortaring to keep out the wet. The West Tarring cottage is an instance of a stone roofing.

❤❤

TIG BRIDGE
painted 1887

Here the white ray'd anemone is born,
Wood-sorrel, and the varnish'd buttercup;
And primrose in its purfled green swathed up,
Pallid and sweet round every budding thorn.
William Allingham

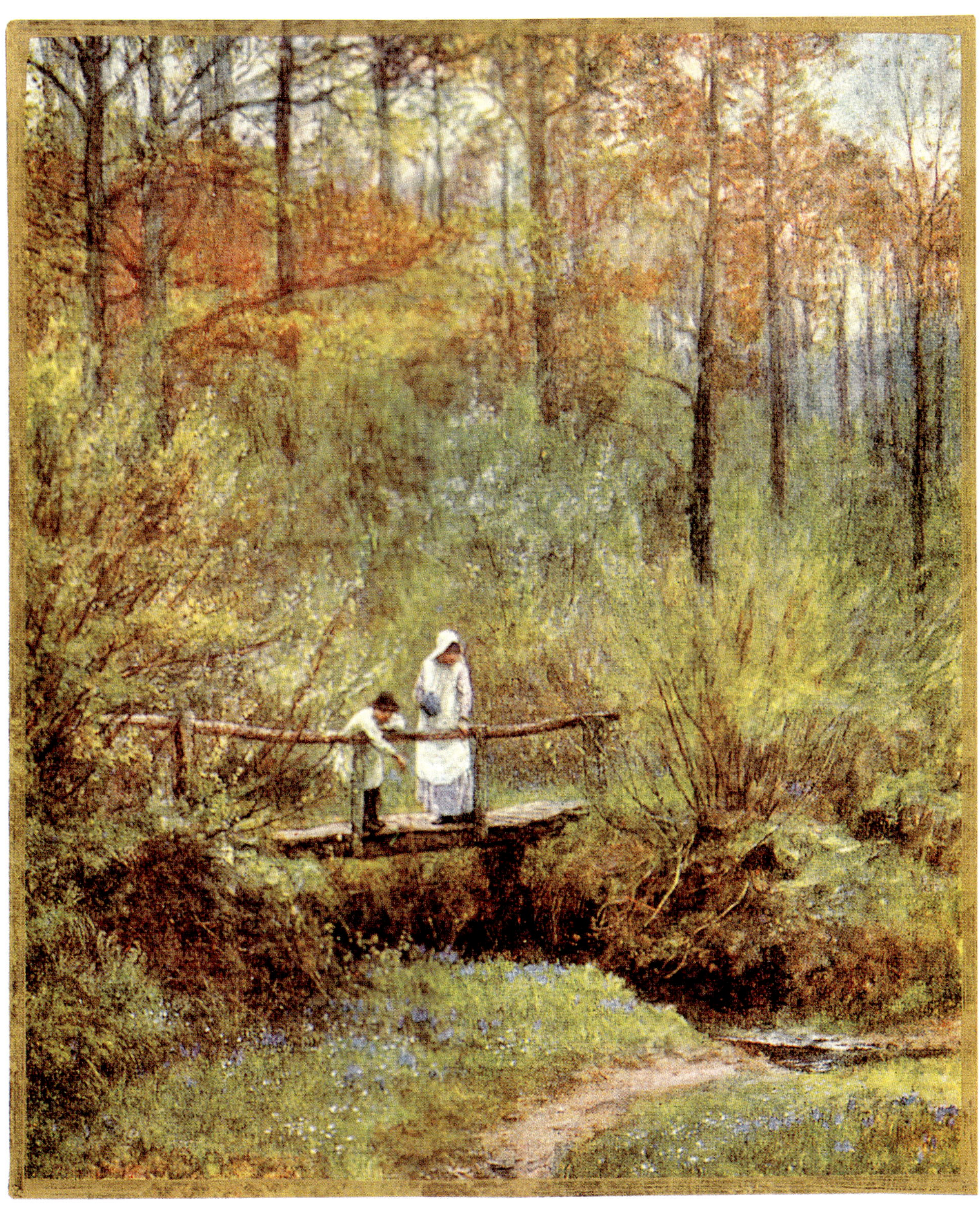

The most usual roof covering was naturally the red tile, for these could be made locally wherever there was brick-earth or clay. They were made thicker and less carefully than modern tiles and the accuracy of Helen Allingham's depiction of them may be detected in almost any of her work by examining where the weight has swagged away the tiles between the main roof beams. One of the charms of an old cottage roof is its irregularity of tile line, owing to the holes for the pegs which hold the tiles not having been accurately placed in each one.

The old solidly built chimney seen in many of Mrs. Allingham's cottages is worthy of note as a type of many sturdy examples which have resisted the ravages of time, and have stood for centuries almost without need of repair. In old days the chimney was regarded not only as a special feature but as an ornament, and not as a necessary but ugly excrescence. Although probably it only served for one room in the house, that service was an important one, and so materials were liberally used in its construction. The variety of plan adopted is almost endless, and the utmost ingenuity seems to have been exerted in its arrangement.

The chimneys are placed generally at either end of the cottage, or they rise in a mass from the centre of the roof; and as if these old builders disliked too much uniformity, we notice, when the latter plan is adopted, various projections, many without apparent reason, except the love of novelty and change. In Kent and Sussex many of the chimneys were of brick, although the house and the base of the chimney-stack were of stone. This arose from the stone not lending itself to thin slabs, and consequently being altogether too cumbrous and bulky. These old chimneys, simple as they were, and built of plain bricks, invariably excited a feeling of admiration, for there was a breadth and sense of proportion about them sadly lacking in cottage chimneys of any later period

THE APPLE ORCHARD
painted1877

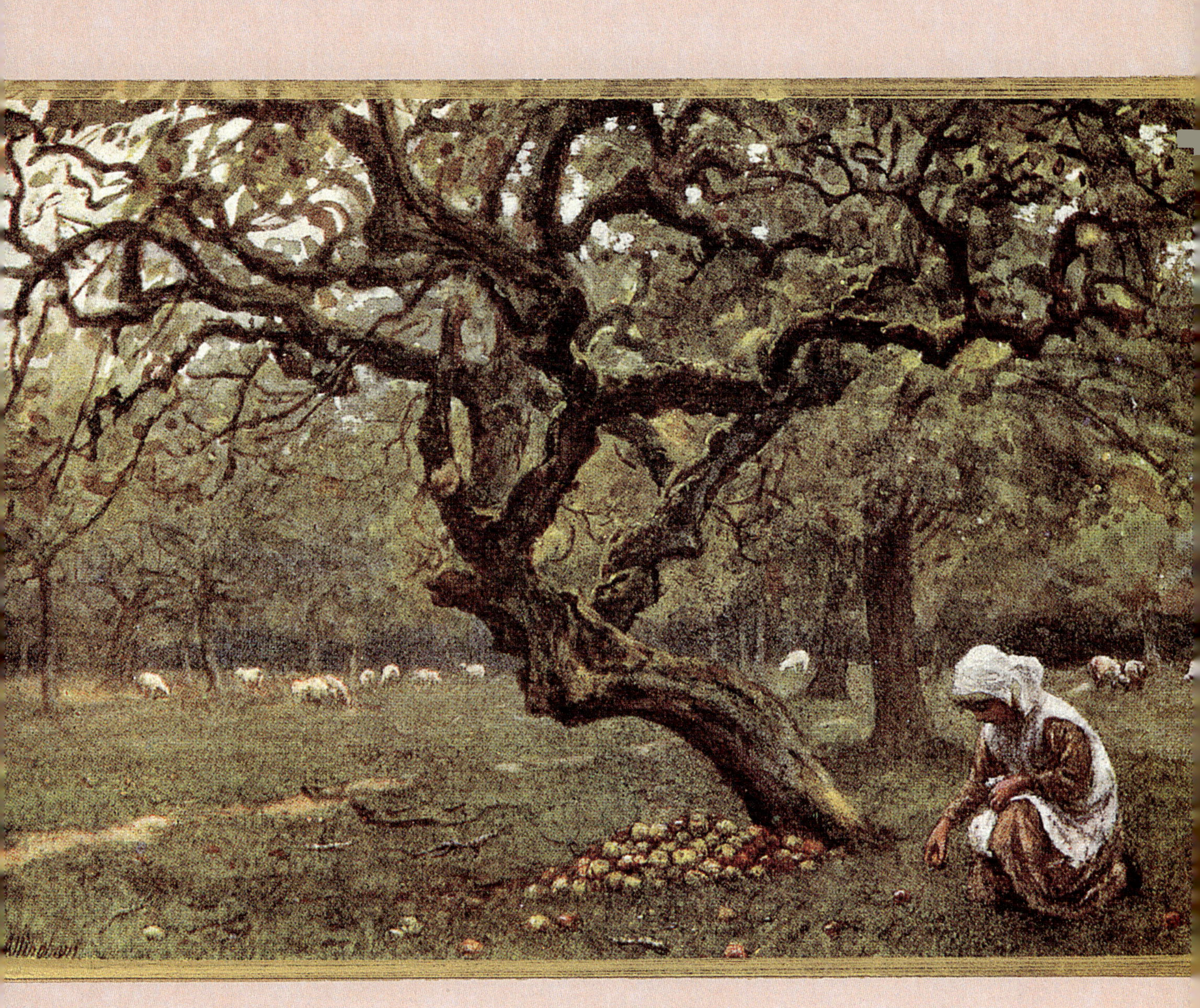

The windows in the old cottages were naturally small when glass was a luxury, and became fewer in number when a tax upon light was one of the means for carrying on wars. They were usually filled with the smallest panes, fitted into lead lattice, so that breakages might be reduced to the smallest area. Not much of this remains, but a specimen of it is to be seen in the Old Buckinghamshire House. One of the few alterations that Mrs. Allingham allowed herself was the substitution of these diamond lattices throughout a house where she found a single example in any of the lights, or if, as she found on more than one occasion, they had been replaced by others and were themselves stacked up as rubbish. She had in her studio some that had been served in this way and which then became useful models.

One might have imagined that the sense of pride in these, the last traces of their village ancestors, would have prompted their descendants, whether of the same kin or not, to deal reverently with them and endeavour to hand on as long as possible these silent witnesses to the honest workmanship of their forbears. Such, unfortunately, is seldom the case. If anyone had visited Witley with this book in his hand and compared the state of the few examples given there, not twenty years after they were painted, he would have seen what was taking place not only in that little village but through the length and breadth of England. It would be perhaps a low estimate to say that a thousand ancient cottages were disappearing in England every year, without trace or record left – many that Shakespeare might have seen, some Chaucer; while the number 'done up' was beyond computation.

The baronial halls have had abundant recognition and praise at the hands of the historian and the painter; the numerous manor-houses, less pretentious, often more lovely, very little; the old cottages next to none, even the local chronicler running his spectacles over them without a pause.

❤❤

CUTTING CABBAGES
painted 1884

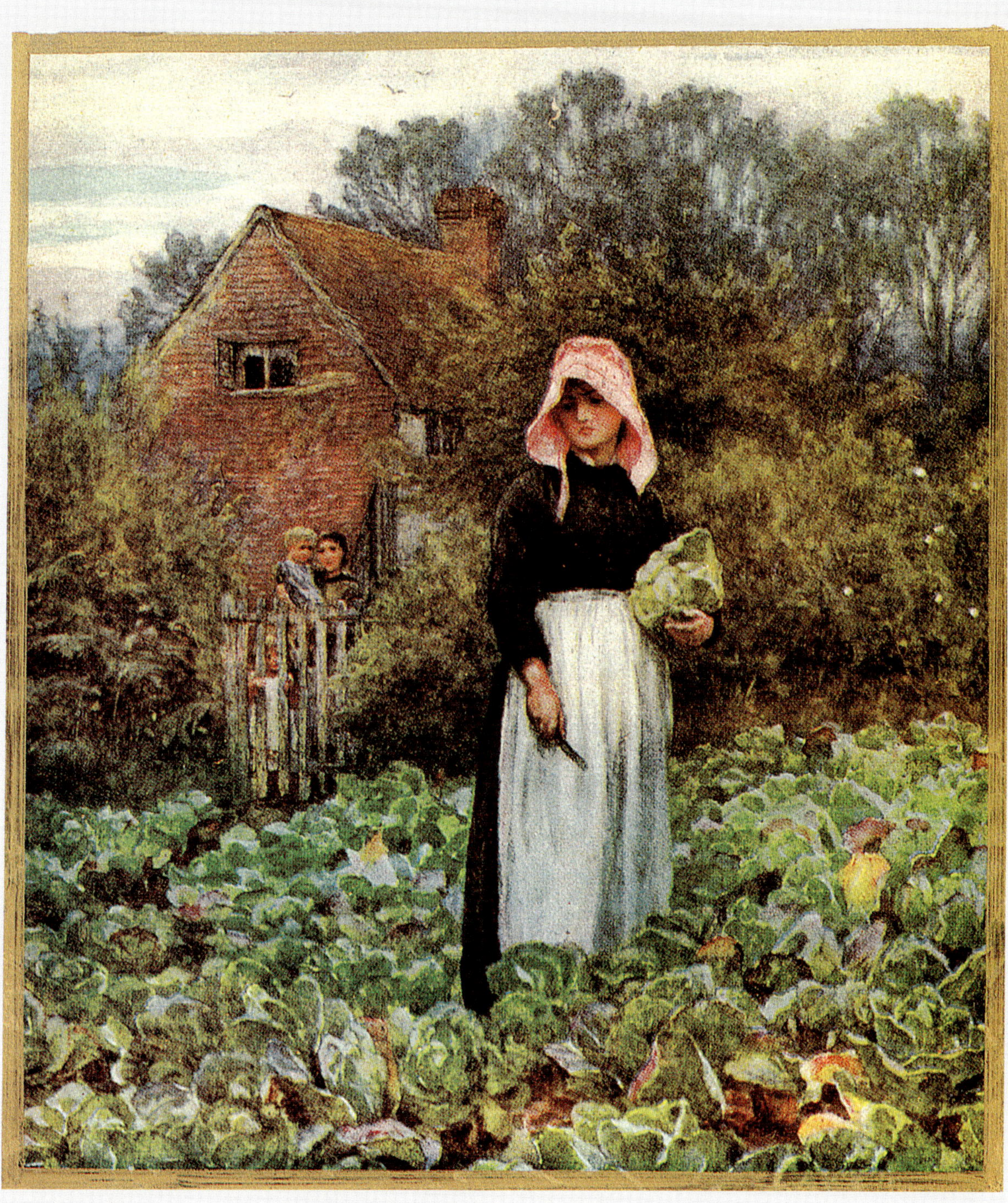

Had Mrs. Allingham done nothing else for her country, she justified her career as a recorder of this altogether overlooked phase of English architecture – a phase that will soon be a thing of the past.

Another painter of the period recorded once being accosted by a bystander in Angers in northern France, as he was wrestling with the perspective of a beautiful old house, with the remark, 'Ah, you had better hurry more than you are doing and finish the roof of that house, for it will be off tomorrow and the whole down in three days.' That was often the case with Mrs. Allingham. More than once a cottage painted one summer disappeared before the painting was exhibited the following spring. Year in year out the process was at work during the quarter of a century during which she produced these work, and it almost came to a joke that were she to paint for another twenty-five years, she might have to cease from lack of material.

♥♥

STUDY OF LEEKS

painted 1902

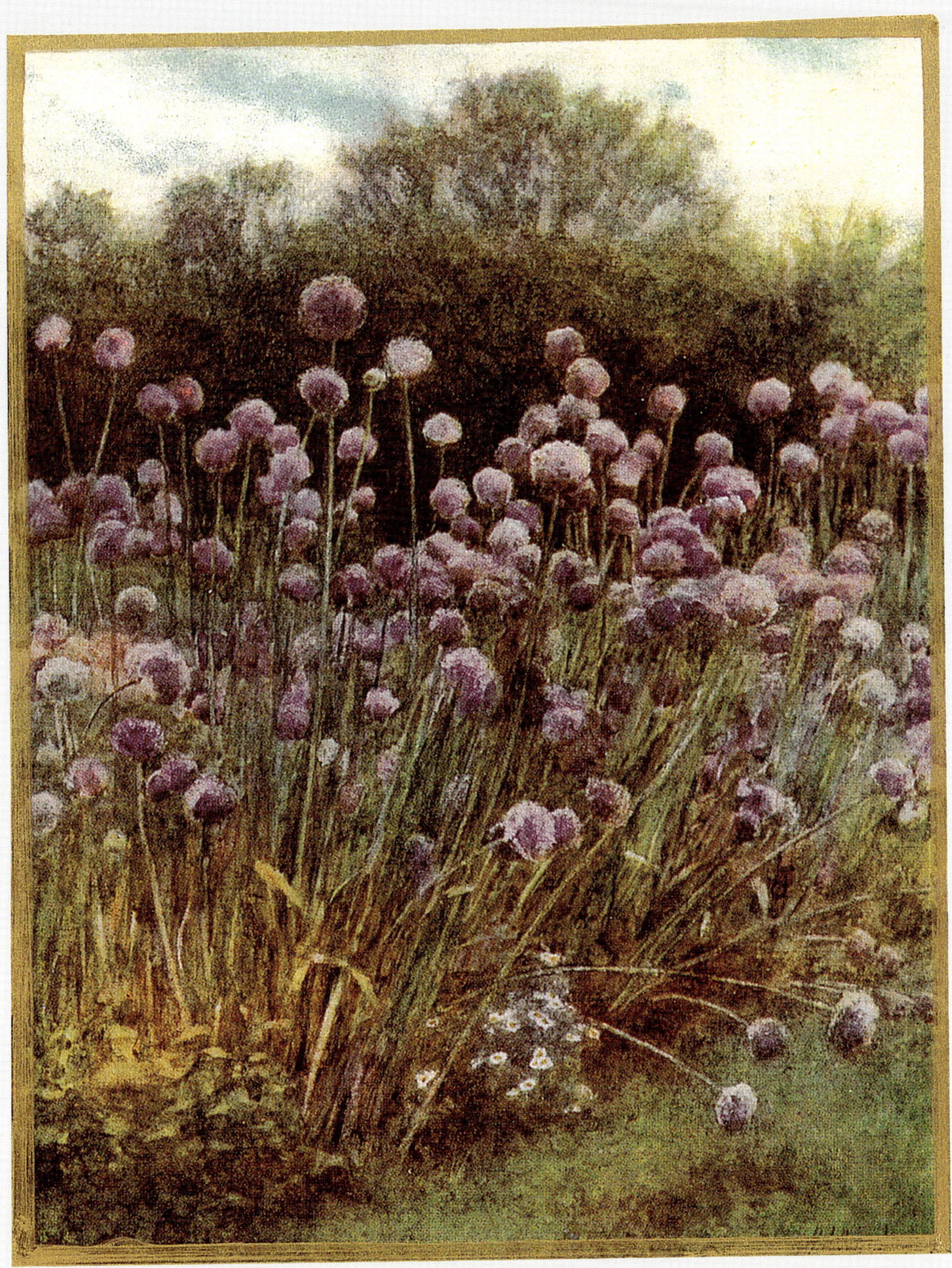

GARDENS AND ORCHARDS

One is nearer God's heart in a garden
Than anywhere else on earth.

When Mrs. Allingham first embarked on this aspect of her Art, the practice of painting gardens was almost as recent an innovation as that of women painting for a living. The Flemish of the fifteenth century, it is true, introduced in a delightful fashion conventional borders of flowers into some of their pictures, probably because they felt that ornament must be presented from end to end of them, and that they do this no better than by adding the gaiety of flowers to their foregrounds. But all through the later dreary days no one touched the garden, for the conglomeration of flowers in the pieces by the Dutchmen of the seventeenth century cannot be regarded as such. Flowers certainly flourished in the gardens of the well-to-do in England in the century between 1750 and 1850, but none of those who executed the paintings of noblemen or of gentlemen's seats which were produced in such quantities during that period ever condescended to introduce them.

VALEWOOD FARM
painted 1903

Valewood was over the ridge which protects Haslemere on the south, and was a very pretty vale of sloping meadows fringed with wood, all under the shadow of Blackdown, to which it belongs. The farm was distinguished from most houses thereabouts in boasting a stream, the headwater of a string of ponds, whence starts the river Wey northwards on its tortuous journey round the western slopes of Hindhead in Surrey. When this was painted, the house was inhabited by well-to-do yeomen and the dairying and milking were still carried out by milkmaids.

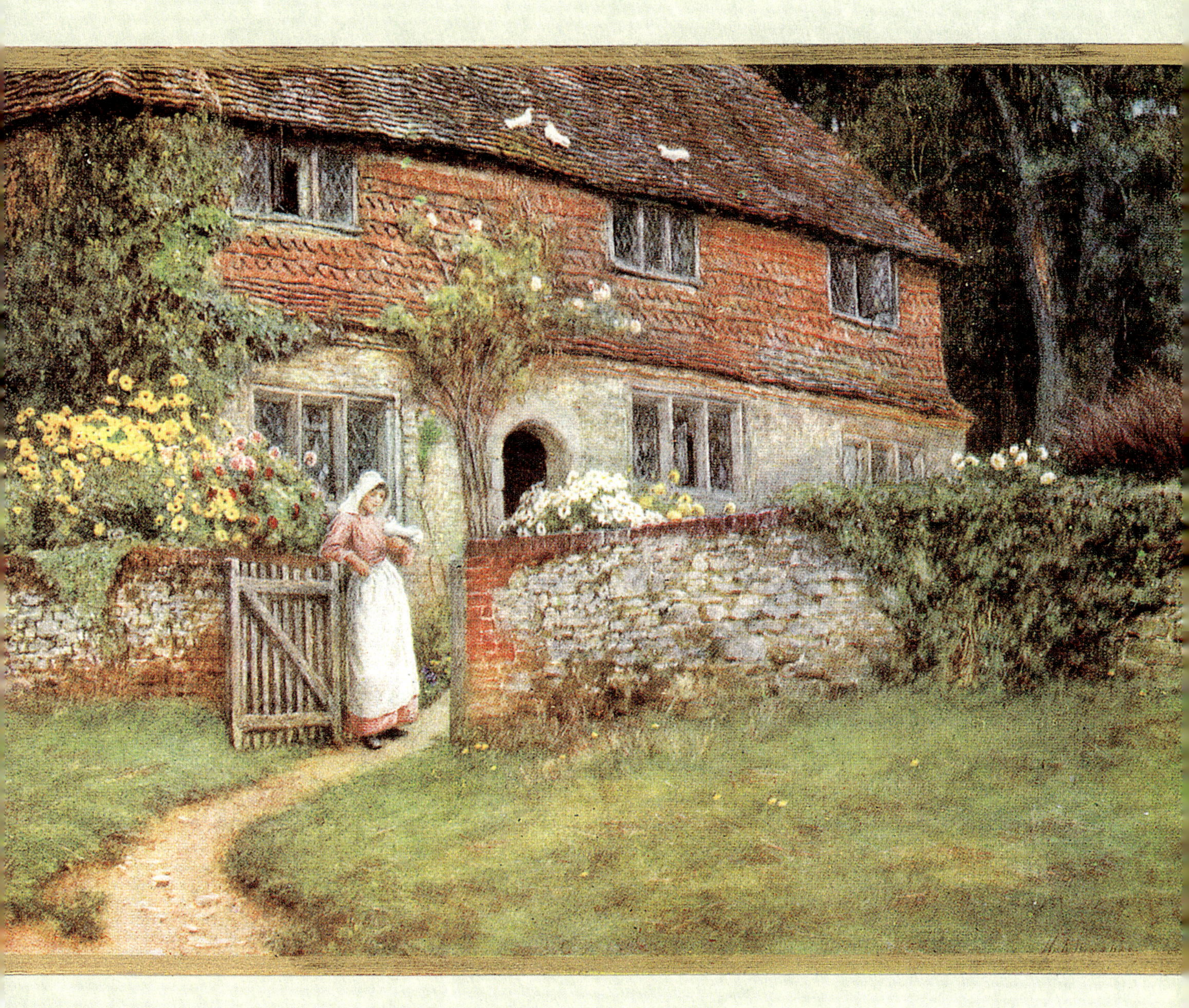

Even as late as 1850, to judge from the titles in its catalogue, the Royal Academy Exhibition did not contain a single specimen of a flower-garden. The only probable one is a picture entitled 'Cottage Roses' ,and any remotely connected with the garden appear under such headings as 'Early Tulips', 'Geraniums', 'Japonicas and Orchids', 'Will you have this pretty rose, Mamma?' or 'The Last Currants of Summer'! Taste only half a century earlier than the time with which this memoir deals was different from what it was in Mrs. Allingham's day, and asked for other provender. Thus, the original owner of the catalogue from which these statistics were taken was an energetic amateur critic, who commended, or otherwise, almost every picture, commendations being signified by crosses and disapproval by noughts. The only work with five crosses is one illustrating the line, 'Now stood Eliza on the wood-crown'd height'. On the other hand, Millais' 'Peace Concluded' stands at the head of the bad marks with five, his 'Blind Girl' with two, which number is shared with Leighton's 'Triumph of Music', Holman Hunt's 'Scapegoat', in addition to being awarded four bad marks, is described as 'detestable and profane'.

These pre-Raphaelites – Millais, Holman Hunt and their followers – then so little esteemed, may in truth be said to have been the originators of the 'garden-drawing cult', chief amongst their followers being Frederick Walker. To the example of the last-named more especially are due the production of the numerous artists – good, bad and indifferent – who seized upon a delightful subject and almost nauseated the public with their productions. The omission of gardens from the painter's *rôle* in later times may to a certain extent have been due to the gardens themselves, or, to speak more correctly, to those under whose charge they were maintained. The ideal of a garden to the true artist must always have differed from that of the professional gardener as to its ordering, even in the days of which I write when the edict had recently gone forth that Nature was to be allowed a hand in the planning.

❦❦

A KENTISH FARMYARD
painted 1900

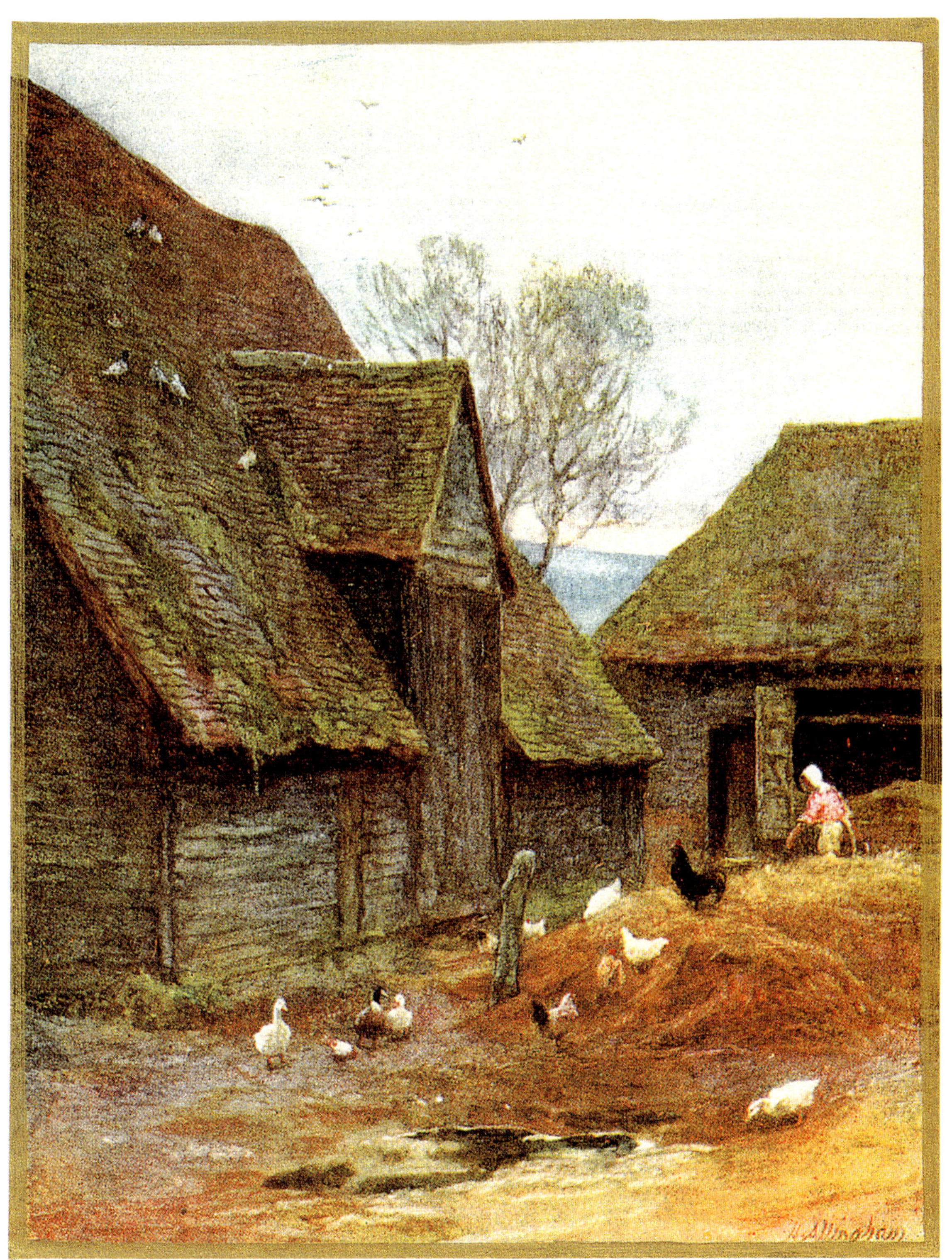

The gardener, no matter whether the surroundings favoured a formal garden or not, insisted upon his harmonies or contrasts of brilliant colourings. If he took these from a manual on gardening he would adopt what is termed a procession of colouring somewhat as follows: strong blues, pale yellow, pink, crimson, strong scarlet, orange and bright yellow. He was told that his colours were to be placed with careful deliberation and forethought, as a painter might employ them in his picture, and not dropped down as he has them on his palette!

Alfred Parsons, a near-contemporary of Mrs. Allingham's and fellow member of the Society of Painters in Water Colours, and George Elgood, the painter of flower-gardens *par excellence*, on occasions grappled with creations such as these, when they were placed in settings of yew-trimmed hedges, or as surroundings of a central statue, or sundial; but it is difficult to say that the results were as successful as those where formality was merely a suggestion and Nature had her say and her way.

Surroundings must, of course, play a prominent part in any garden scheme. However much we may dislike a stiff formality, it is sometimes a necessity. For instance, herbaceous plants, with annuals of mixed colours, would look out of place on a lawn in front of an imposing manor house, which calls for a mass of plants of uniform colours. The lie of the ground, too, must in such a case be taken into account; where in front of such a house there is a sloping descent facing towards the sun, it is not easy to keep the soil moist. Geraniums and calceolarias, which stand such conditions, are therefore almost a necessity.

When the possibility of a book containing examples of her work was first proposed to Mrs. Allingham, her chief objection was her certainty that no process could reproduce her paintings satisfactorily. Her method of work was, she believed, entirely opposed to mechanical reproduction, for she employed not only every formula used by her fellow water-colourists, but

❤❤

AN OLD BUCKINGHAMSHIRE HOUSE
painted 1899

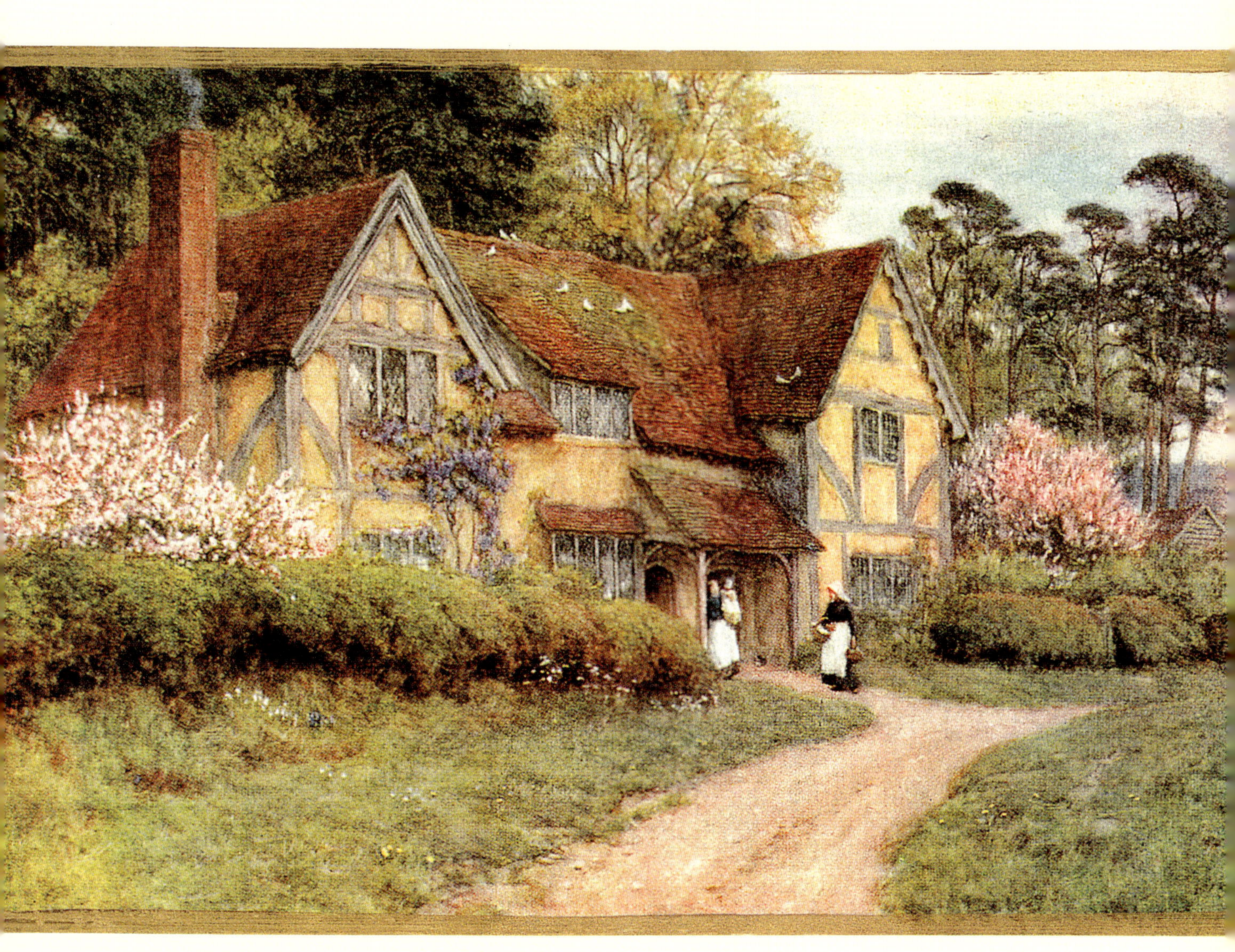

many that others would not venture upon. Amongst those she listed was her system of obtaining effects by rubbing, scrubbing and scratching. But the process was not to be denied, and she was fain to admit that even in these it was possible to achieve a wonderful reproduction.

Nowhere are these methods of Mrs. Allingham's more utilised, and with greater effect, than in her paintings of flower-gardens. The system of painting flowers in masses underwent great changes in the course of her lifetime. The plan generally adopted when she was at the start of her career was to draw and paint first the flowers and then the foliage. This method left the flowers isolated objects and the foliage without substantiality.

Mrs. Allingham's technique was the reverse of this. Take, for instance, the white clove pinks in the foreground of the painting of the kitchen garden at Farringford. These are so admirably done that their perfume almost scents the room. They have been simply carved out of a background of walk and grey-green spikes and left as white paper, all their drawing and modelling being achieved by a dexterous use of the knife and a wetted and rubbed surface. The poppies, roses, columbines and stocks have all been created in the same way. The advantage is seen at once. There are no badly pencilled outlines and the blooms blend amongst themselves and grow naturally out of their foliage.

While extolling Mrs. Allingham's virtuosity with flowers, it also seems apt to draw attention to two of her portrayals of the humble denizens of the kitchen garden. The cabbage is probably to most people the most uninteresting

❦❦

MINNA
painted 1886

This charming picture of a small child, lost in a sea of old-fashioned cottage garden flowers, was painted in Helen Allingham's own garden at Sandhills. Pansies, sea-pinks, marigolds, sweet-williams, snap-dragons, escholtzias and irises grow in profusion against a background of rose bushes.

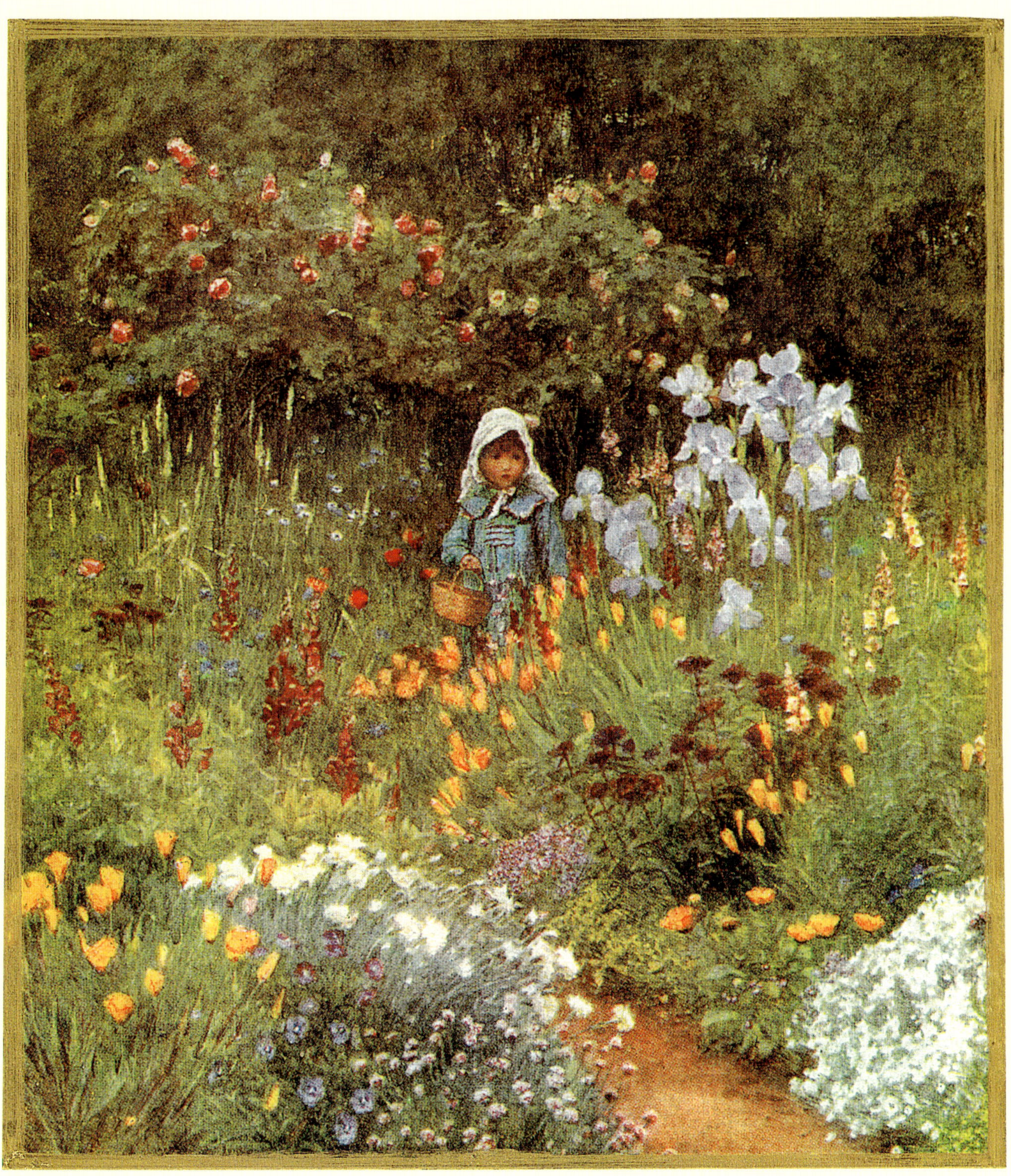

tenant of this part of the garden, and yet its presence there was probably the motive which set Mrs. Allingham to work to make 'Cutting Cabbages', for it is clear that in the first instance it was conceived as a study of the varied and delicate mother-of-pearl hues which each presented to an artistic eye. As a piece of painting it is extremely meritorious through its being absolutely straightforward drawing and brushwork, the highlights being left, and not obtained by the usual method of cutting, scraping or body colour. The buxom mother of a growing family selecting the best plant for their dinner is just the personal note which distinguishes each and every one of the illustrations in this book.

When Mrs. Allingham in wandering round a garden came upon a bed of flowering leeks (see 'Study of Leeks', page 79) and 'singularly moved to love the lovely that are not beloved', at once sat down to paint it in preference to a more ambitious display in the front garden that was at her service, her friends probably considered her artistic perception to be peculiar, and there may be some who will deem that it does not merit the honour given to it by introduction into these pages. But it has more than one claim to recognition here, for it is unusual in subject, delicate in its violet tints, not unbecoming in form, and is here disassociated from the disagreeable odour which usually accompanies the reality.

IN A SUMMER GARDEN
painted 1887

This was painted in almost the same spot in the artist's garden as Minna's portrait shown on page 87.

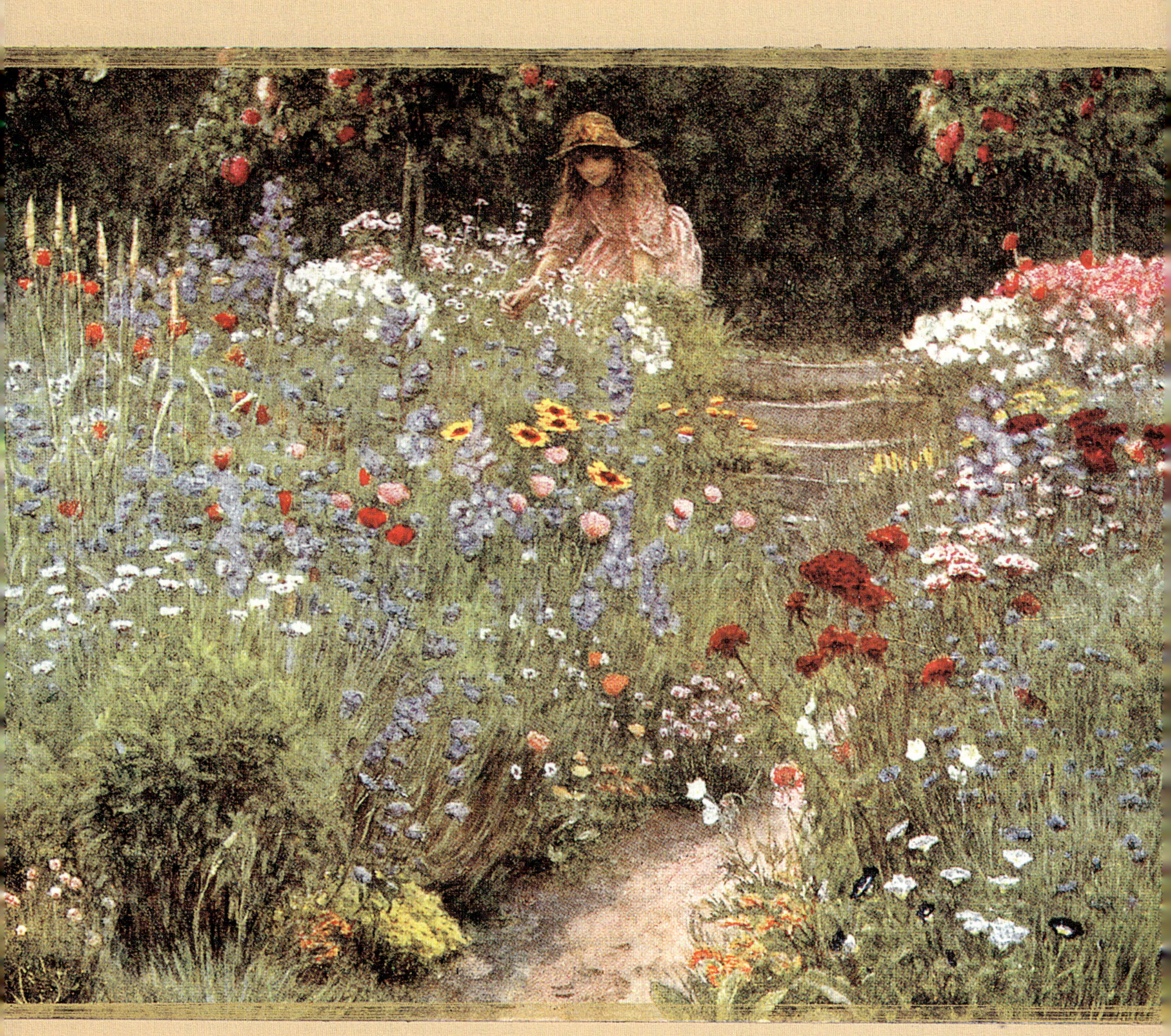

WITH THE POET LAUREATE

Few poets have been so fortunate in their residences as was the great Poet Laureate of the Victorian era in the two which he for many years called his own. Selected in the first instance for their beauty and their seclusion, they had other advantages which fitted them admirably to a poet's temperament.

Farringford, at the western end of the Isle of Wight, was the first to be acquired, being purchased in 1853; it was Tennyson's home for forty years, and he wrote most of his best-known works here. At the time when it came into his hands communication with the mainland was of the most primitive description, and the poet and his wife had to cross the Solent in a rowing-boat. So far removed was he from intrusion there that he could indulge in what to him were favourite pastimes – sweeping up the leaves, mowing the grass, gravelling the walks and digging the beds – without interruption.

Many of the visitors which railway and steamship facilities brought to the neighbourhood in later years felt that he set the boundary within which no foot other than his own and that of his friends should tread at an extreme limit. Golfers over the Needles Links – persons who, perhaps, were prone to consider that whatever could be made into a course should be so utilised – were wont to look with covetous eyes over a portion of the Downs that would have formed a much-needed addition to their course, but over which no ball was allowed to be played. But the pertinacity of the crowd, in endeavouring to get a sight of the Laureate necessitated an inexorable rule if the retreat was to be what it was intended – namely, a place for work and for rest.

❤❤

WALLFLOWERS
painted ca 1893

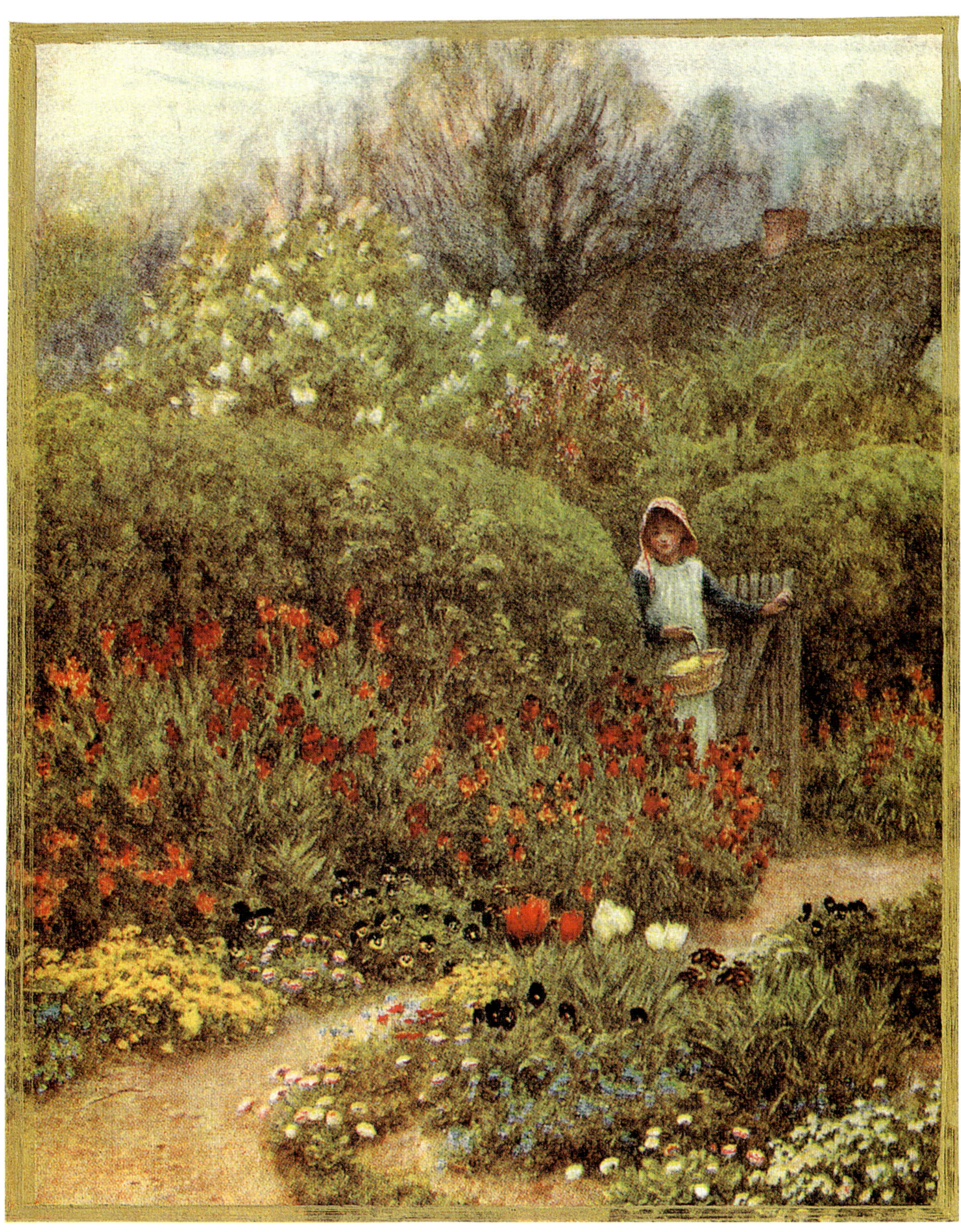

Mrs. Tennyson described 'her wild house amongst the pine trees' thus:

> The golden green of the trees, the burning splendour of Blackgang Chine and the red bank of the primeval river contrasted with the turkis blue of the sea (that is our view from the drawing-room) make altogether a miracle of beauty at sunset. We are glad that Farringford is ours.

Although at times the weather can be cold and bleak in this sheltered corner of the Isle of Wight, and

> The screams of a madden'd beach
> Dragged down by the wave

must often have 'shocked the ear' in Farringford, the climate is too relaxing for continued residence, and Tennyson's second house, Aldworth, was well chosen as a contrast. The Laureate's friend, the Irish poet Aubrey de Vere, thus described it:

> It lifted England's great poet to a height from which he could gaze on a large portion of that English land which he loved so well, see it basking in its most affluent beauty, and only bound by the inviolate sea.

The house stands at an elevation of some six hundred feet above the sea, on the spur of Blackdown, which is the highest ground in Sussex, on a steep side towards the Weald, just where the greensand hills break off. It is some two miles from Haslemere, and just within the Sussex border.

Mrs. Allingham painted the house at Farringford in the spring, when the lawn was pied with daisies and the Laureate required his heavy cloak to

❧❧

THE CONDEMNED COTTAGE
painted 1902

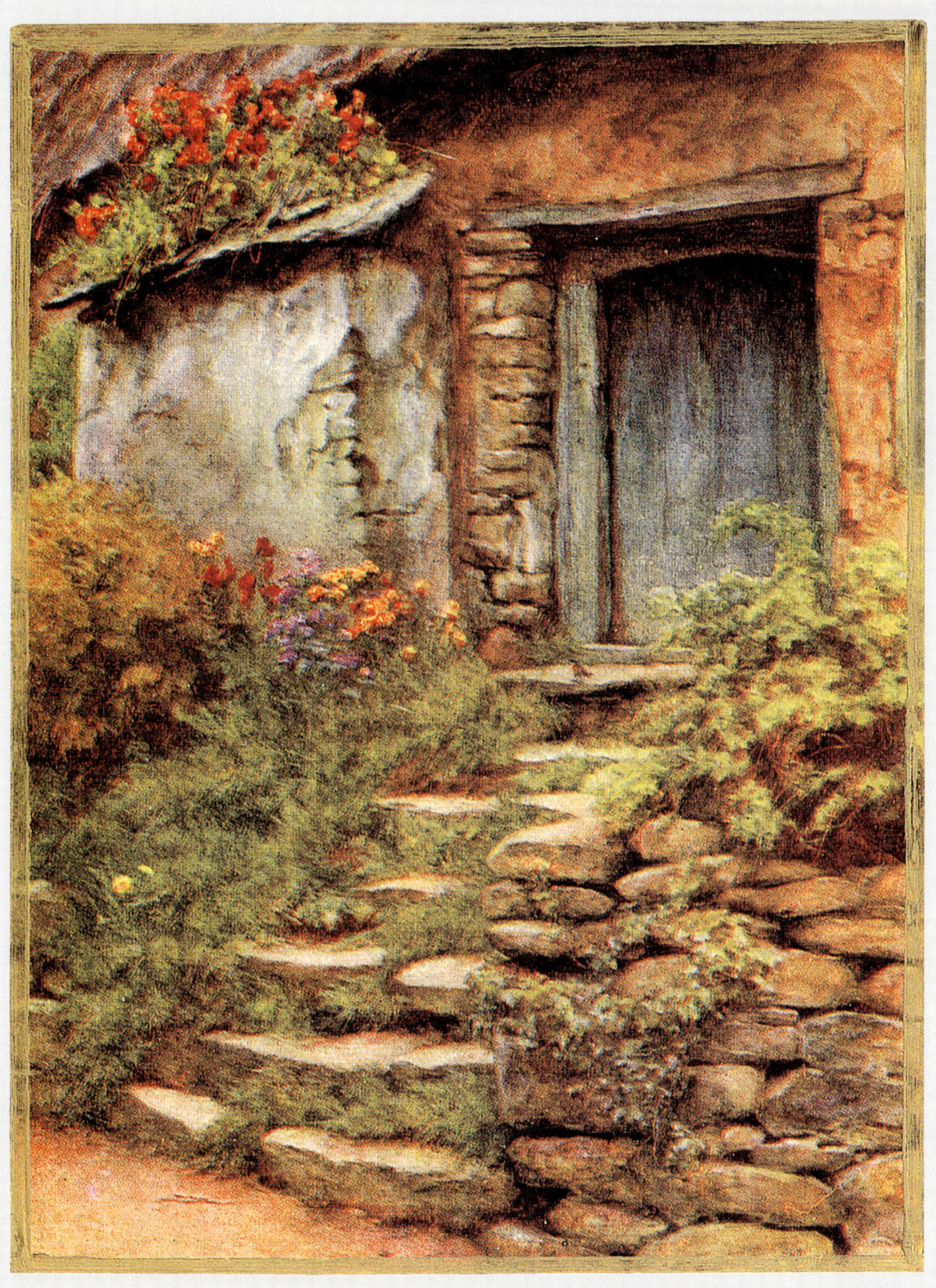

guard him from the keenness of the April winds. The kitchen garden at Farringford, which somewhat belied its name, for flowers encroached everywhere upon the vegetables and the apple trees rose amidst a parterre of blossom, was painted in its summer aspect.

The kitchen garden at Aldworth opened up a very different prospect to the banked-up background of trees at Farringford. Standing at a very considerable elevation, it commanded a magnificent view over the Weald of Sussex.

It was rare for Mrs. Allingham to set her flowers so near the horizon as in this case, but no doubt the same feeling that appealed to the poet's eye, and impelled him to pen the lines quoted in the caption on page 96, fascinated the artist's – namely, the beautiful appearance of the varied hues of flowers against a background of delicate blue.

In this work, painted in October, the apple tree has already shed most of its leaves, the hollyhock stems are baring and autumnal flowers, in which yellow so much predominates, as, for instance, the great marigold, the herbaceous sunflower and the calliopsis, are much in evidence. Nasturtiums and every free-growing creeper have long ago trailed their stems over the box edging and make an untidiness which forebodes their early destruction at the hands of the gardener. Of sweet-scented flowers only a few peas and mignonette remain.

THE HOUSE, FARRINGFORD
painted 1890

William Allingham, the artist's husband, had long been a friend of the then Poet Laureate, Alfred, Lord Tennyson. Helen Allingham was introduced to him soon after her marriage and she and her husband were frequent visitors to Aldworth, the house which the Tennysons had purchased in 1853 and which was to be their residence for forty years. Farringford is situated at the western end of the Isle of Wight. The house is shown in spring when the lawn was pied with daisies.

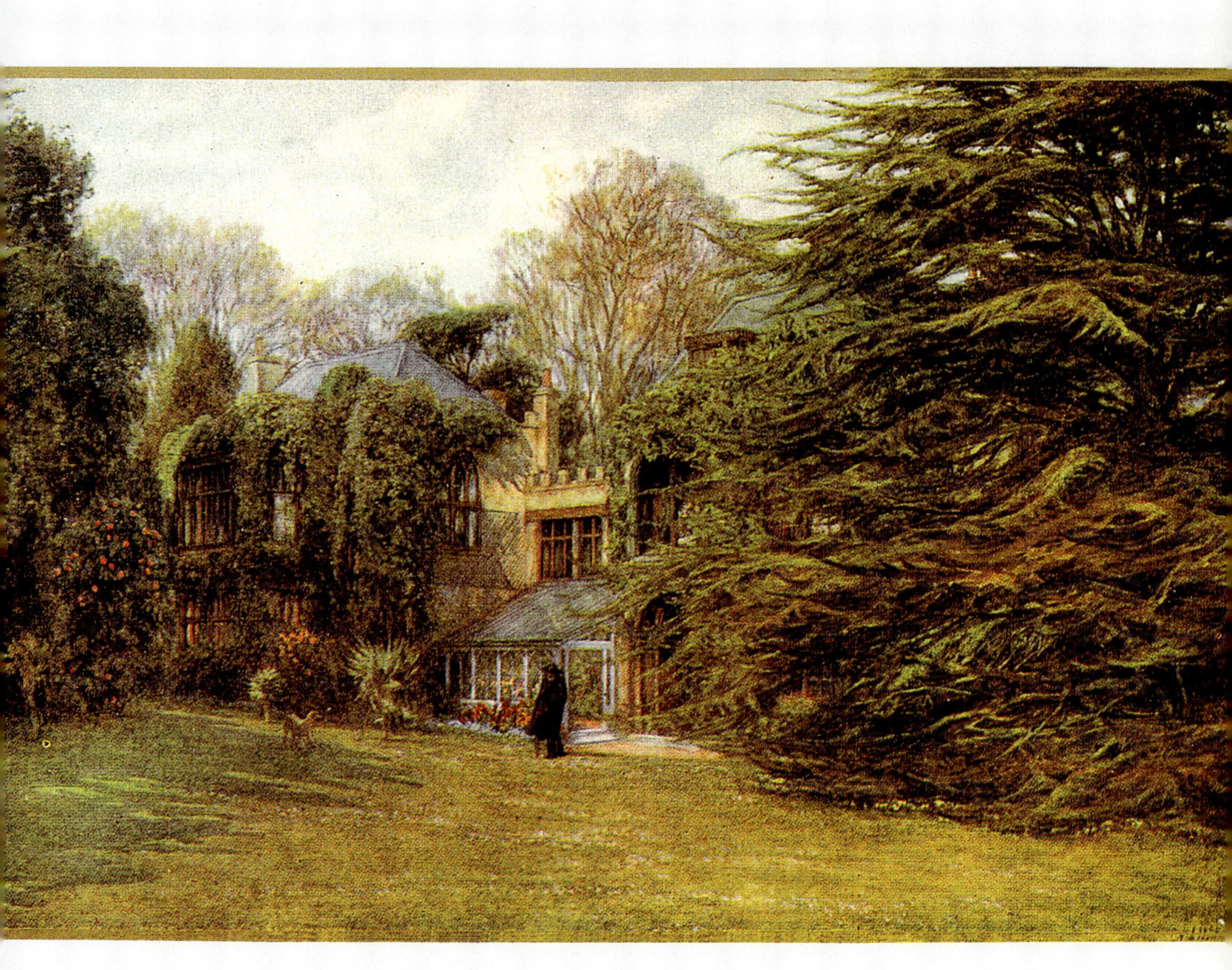

Mr. Allingham knew the Poet Laureate for many years, having at one time lived at Lymington, which was the point of departure for the western end of the Isle of Wight, and whence he often crossed to Farringford. The artist's first meeting with Tennyson was soon after her marriage. He and his son Hallam had come up to town and had walked over from Clapham, where they were staying, to Chelsea. He invited Mrs. Allingham to Aldworth, an invitation which was accepted shortly afterwards. The poet was very proud of the country which framed his house, and during this visit he took her on his special walks to Blackdown, to Fir Tree Corner (whence there is a wide view over the Weald towards the sea) and to a great favourite of his, the Foxes' Hole, a lovely valley beyond his own grounds. Whilst on this last-named ramble he suddenly turned round and chided the artist for 'chattering instead of looking at the view'. During this visit he read to her a part of his *Harold*, and the wonder of his voice and whole manner of reading or chanting were things she never forgot.

When the Allinghams went to live at Witley they were able to get to and from Aldworth in an afternoon and so were frequent visitors there. One day in the

♥♥

A Garden in October, Aldworth
painted 1891

Tennyson loved the house and the views surrounding it. He immortalised this part of the country in the poem entitled 'Roses on the Terrace':
Green Sussex, fading into blue,
With one glimpse of the sea.
It was this view that the dying poet longed to see once again on his last morning when he cried: 'I want the blinds up! I want to see the sky and the light!'
Helen Allingham's painting was done on a rainy October day and there is a record that even two umbrellas could not prevent her getting wet through. October is the saddest time for the garden, and whatever can be gleaned is often more precious than the full abundance of summer.

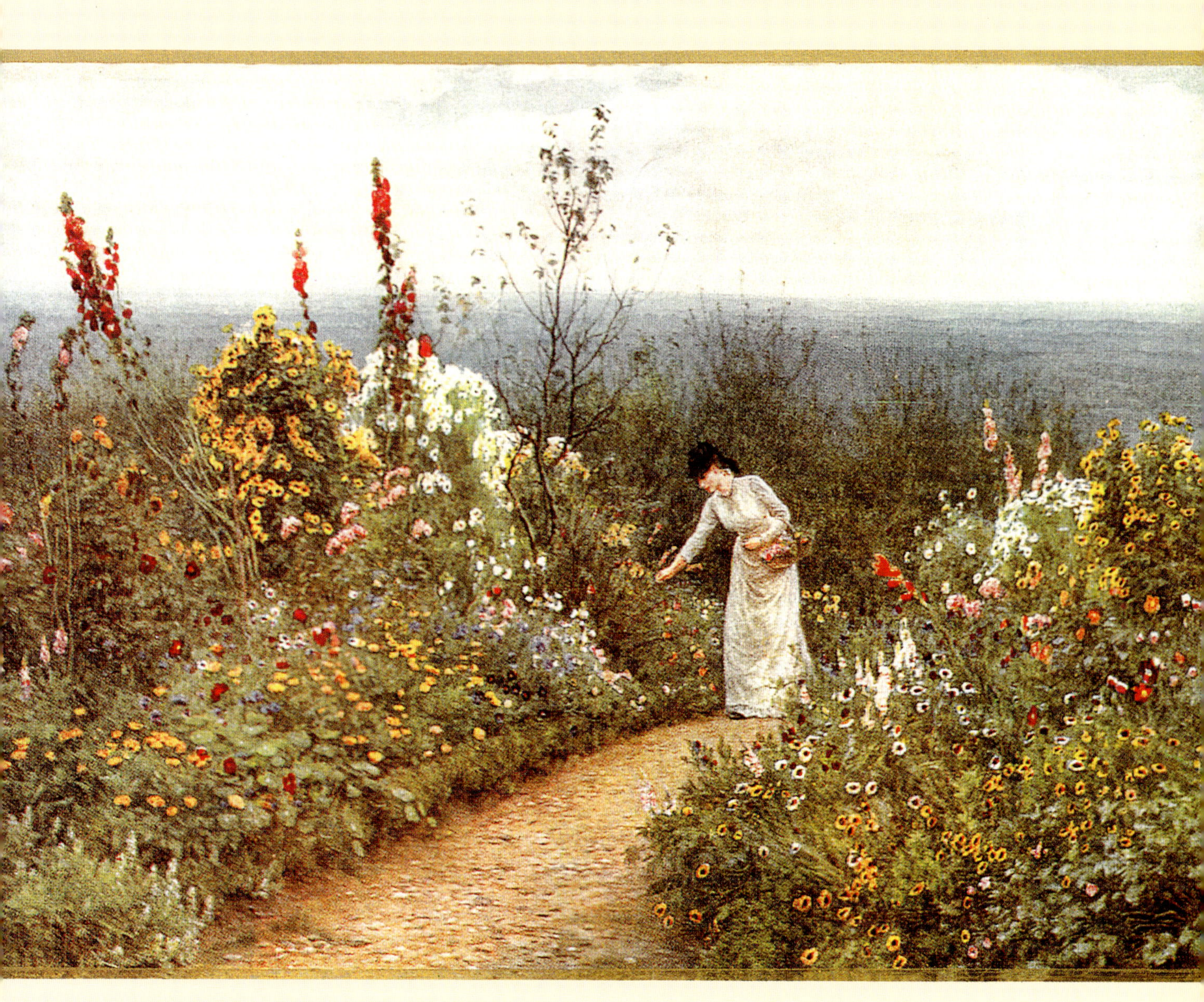

autumn of 1881 Mrs. Allingham went over alone, owing to her husband's absence, and after lunch the poet walked with her to Foxes' Hole, where they sat on bundles of pea-sticks, she painting an old cottage since pulled down, and he watching her. After a time he said slowly, 'I should like to do that. It does not look very difficult.' Years later he showed her some water-colour paintings he had made, from imagination, of Mount Ida clad in dark fir groves, which she thought remarkably clever in the way they suggested what he wished to convey.

Lord Tennyson's Isle of Wight home Mrs. Allingham did not see until after she returned to live in London, when Mr. Hallam Tennyson, in conversing with her about her paintings, told her that if she would come to the Isle of Wight he could show her some fine old cottages. She accordingly went, at Easter 1890, to Freshwater, across the Yar valley from Farringford, when he was as good as his word, and she at once began paintings of 'The Dairy' and the cottage 'At Pound Green'. Miss Kate Greenaway, who had come to stay with her, also painted the same subjects. The next spring, and for many springs afterwards, Mrs. Allingham went to Freshwater, generally after the Easter holidays.

During one of these stays she accompanied Birket Foster to Farringford, and the poet asked the two artists to come for a walk with him. There happened to be a boy of the party in a sailor costume with a bright blue collar and a

❦❦

THE KITCHEN-GARDEN, FARRINGFORD
painted 1894

The term 'kitchen-garden' was a slight misnomer here, as garden flowers encroached everywhere upon the vegetables and, in summer, when this view was painted, delphiniums, oriental poppies, stocks and larkspurs made a riot of colour. This was painted four years after the poet's death and Helen Allingham must have remembered how much Tennyson had loved this garden and how he used to come down this path, almost every day, to check the rain-gauge and the barometer.

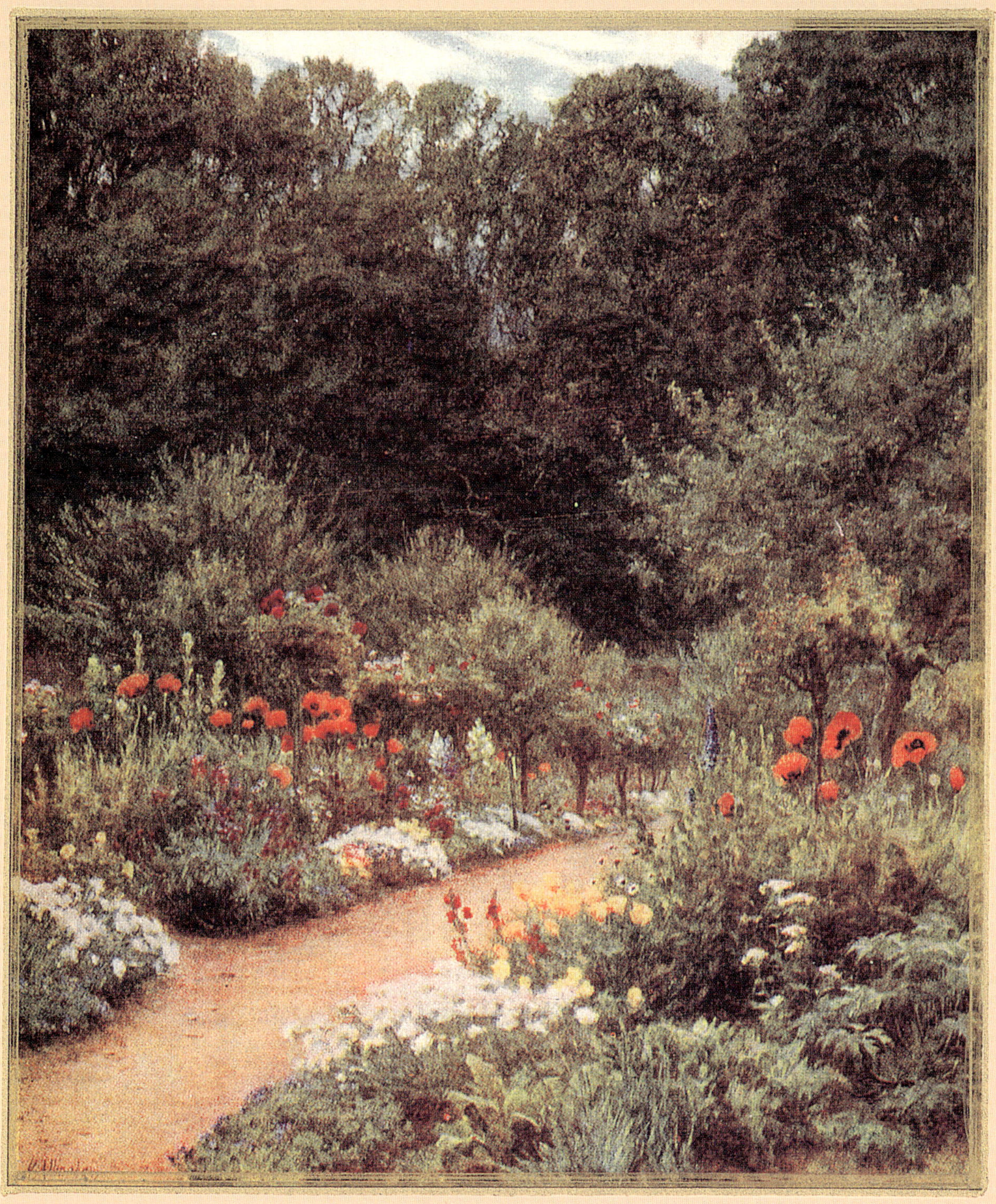

scarlet cap. Birket Foster, who was at the moment walking behind with Mrs. Allingham, said, 'Why is that red and blue so disagreeable?'

Tennyson's quick ear caught something and he turned on them, setting his stick firmly in the ground, and asked Mr. Foster to explain himself.

'Well,' Mr. Foster said, 'I only know that the effect of the contrast is to make cold water run down my spine.'

Mrs. Allingham cordially agreed with Mr. Birket Foster, but Tennyson could not feel the 'cold water', although he saw their point, and said it was doubtless with painters as with himself in poetry, namely, that some combinations of sound gave intense pleasure, whilst others grated, and he quoted certain lines as being so to him.

On another occasion, whilst they were walking together at Freshwater, he said something which led Mrs. Allingham to mention that she generally kept her paintings by her for a long time, often for years, working on them now and again and pondering over figures and incidents for them. (Indeed, Mrs. Allingham's friends sometimes said to her, 'You paint so quickly.' Her reply was, 'Perhaps I make a quick beginning, but I take a long time to finish.') Tennyson remarked that it was the same in the case of poems, and that he used generally to keep his by him, often in print, for a considerable time before publishing.

❤❤

THE DAIRY, FARRINGFORD
painted 1890

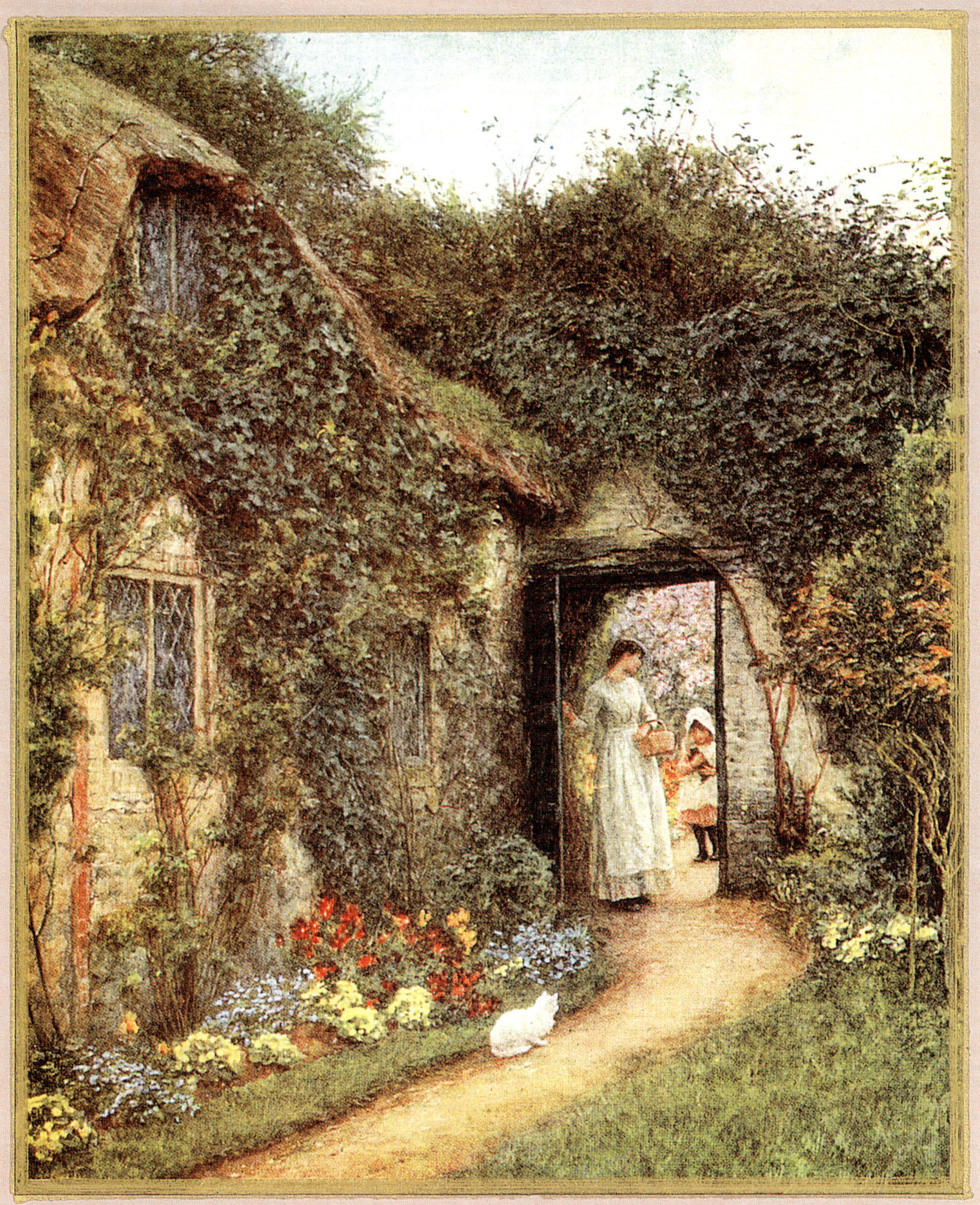

THE ARTIST IN HER TIME

That a true artist is always individual, and that his or her work is always affected by some one or other of his predecessors or contemporaries, would appear to be a paradox; nevertheless it is a proposition that few will dispute. Art has been practised for too long a period and by too many talented people, for entirely novel views or treatments of Nature to be possible, and whilst an artist may be entirely unaware that he has imbibed anything from others, it is certain that if he has had eyes to see he must have done so.

Mrs. Allingham's work, whether in subject or execution, was, so far as she was aware, entirely her own, and it would, perhaps, be sufficient to leave the matter after having placed that assertion on record. However, comparisons have been made between her work and that of certain other artists, so it may be appropriate to deal with them here.

The two names with whose productions those of Mrs. Allingham are most frequently linked are Frederick Walker and Birket Foster: the first in connection with her figures, the latter with her cottage subjects. As regards these two artists it must be remembered that both their and her early employment lay in the same direction, namely, that of book illustration, and therefore each started with somewhat similar methods of execution and subject, varied only by leanings towards the style of any work they came in

♥♥

HOOK HILL FARM, FRESHWATER
painted 1891

This old farmhouse on the other side of the Yar Valley, near Farringford, was a favourite destination for Lord Tennyson while out for a walk. It possessed a fine yard and an old thatched barn which Helen Allingham contrived to paint before it was lost for ever.

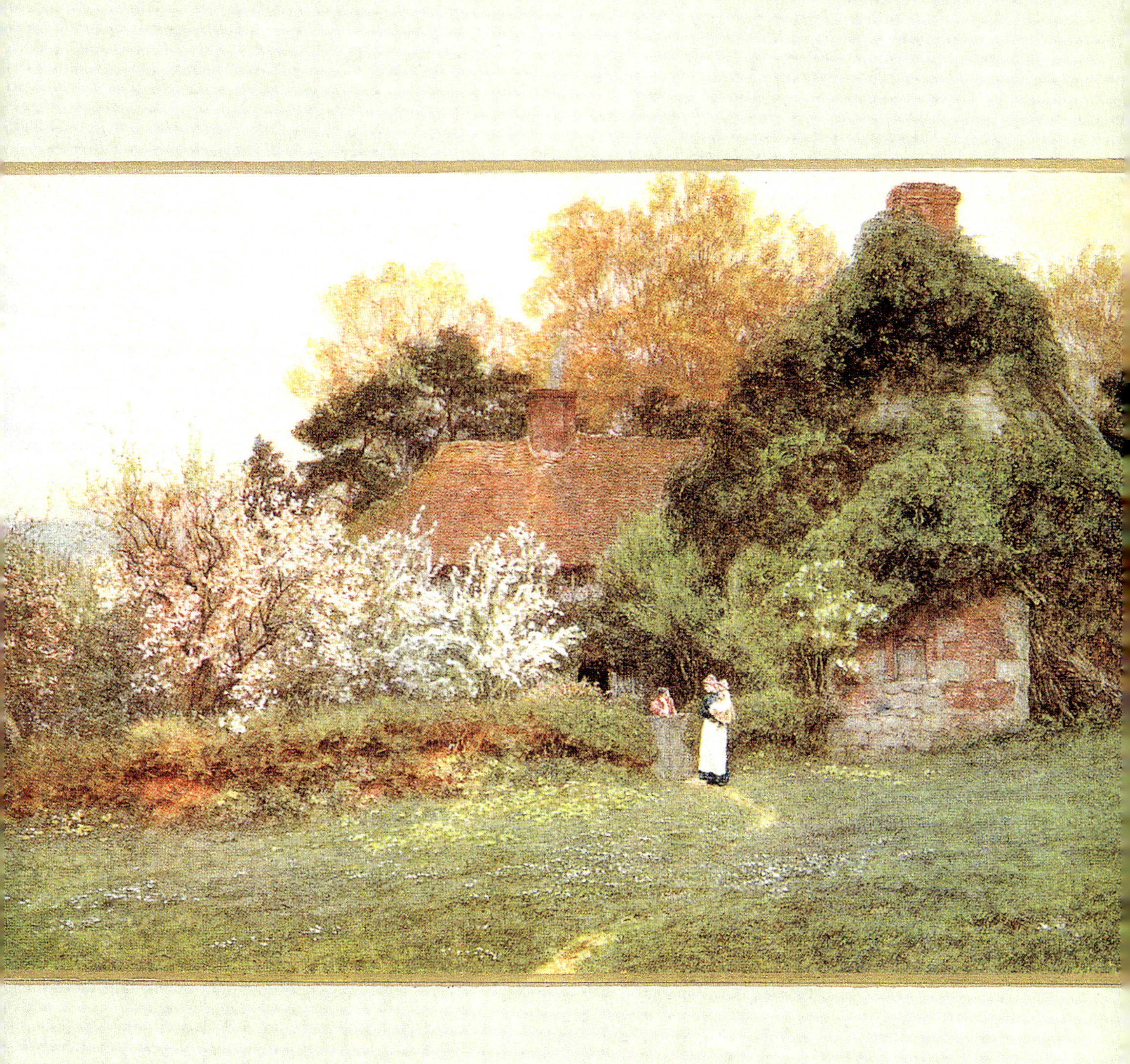

contact with, or by their own individuality. That both had much in common is well known; in fact, Mrs. Allingham used to tell Mr. Foster that she considered him, as did others, the father of Walker and Pinwell.

In the case of Frederick Walker, his career was at its most interesting phase whilst Mrs. Allingham was a student. Her first visit to the Royal Academy was probably in 1868, when his 'Vagrants' was exhibited, to be followed in 1869 by 'The Old Gate', in 1870 by 'The Plough' and in 1872 by 'The Harbour of Refuge'.

It must not be forgotten that the name of Frederick Walker was at this time on everyone's lips – that is, everyone who could be deemed to be included in the small Art world of those days. The painter visitors to the Academy Schools sang his praises to the students, and he himself fascinated and charmed them with his boyish and graceful presence. As Mrs. Allingham said, everybody in the Schools 'adored' him and his work, and on the opening of the Academy doors on the first Monday in May the students rushed to his picture first of all.

To contradict a maxim of Walker's in those days was the rankest heresy in a student. Mrs. Allingham remembered an occasion when another painter was holding forth on the right methods of water-colour work, asserting that the paper should be put flat down on a table, as was the custom with the old men, and the colour should be laid on in washes and left to dry with edges. If Walker taught any other method, asserted this unnamed rival, he was wrong. Mrs. Allingham and her fellow-students were furious at their hero being possibly at fault, and asked for the opinion of an Academician. His reply was: 'And *who* is Mr. —, and how does *he* paint that *he* should lay down the law? If Walker *is* all wrong with his methods, he paints like an angel.'

❤❤

ONE OF LORD TENNYSON'S COTTAGES, FARRINGFORD
painted 1900

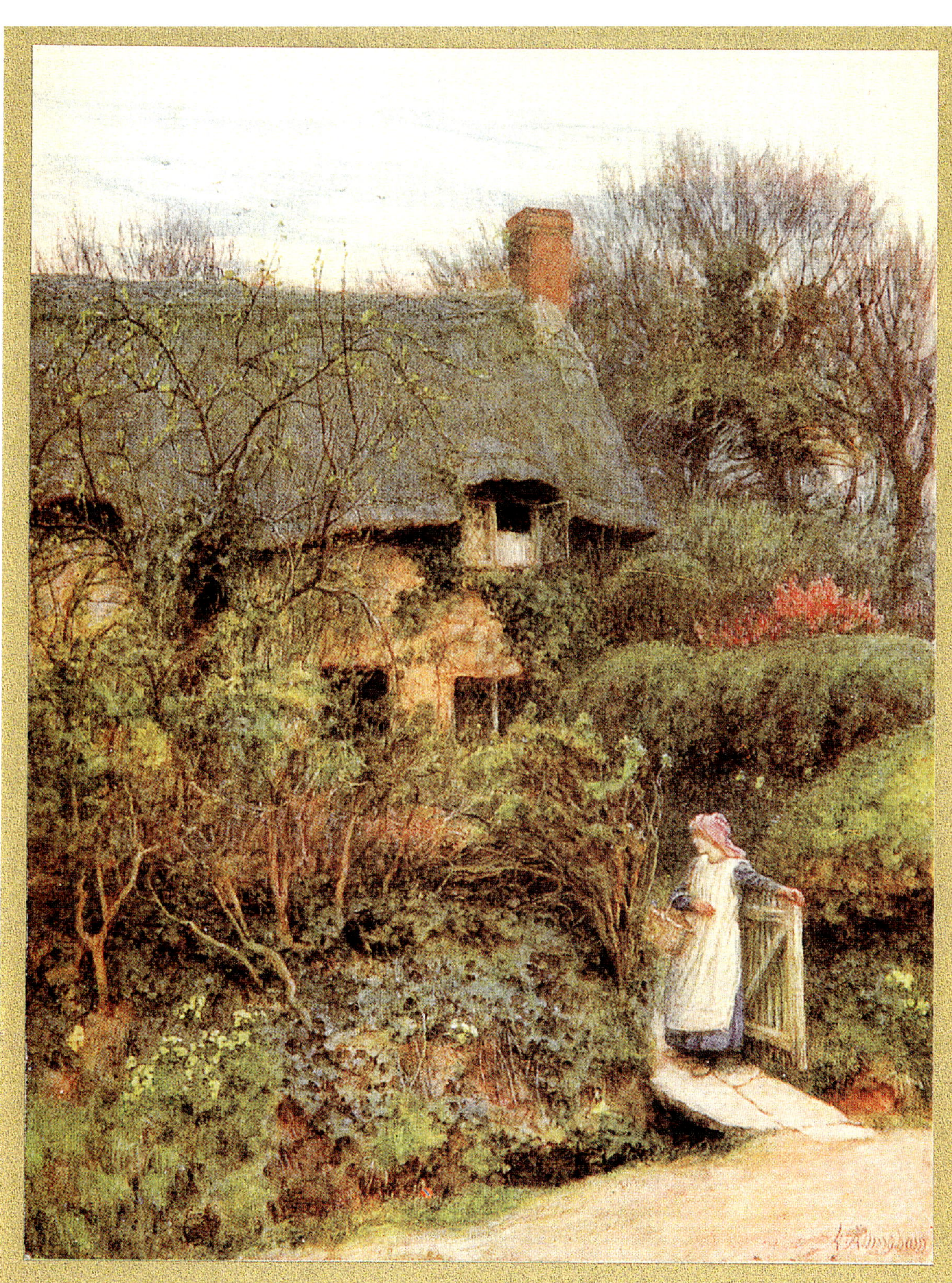

Mrs. Allingham's confession of faith was this:

> I *was* influenced, doubtless, by his work. I adored it, but I never
> consciously copied it. It revealed to me certain beauties and aspects
> of Nature, as du Maurier's had done, and as North's and others
> have since done, and then I saw like things for myself in Nature,
> and painted them, I truly think, in my own way – not the best way,
> I dare say, but in the only way *I* could.

Those critics, therefore, who discover not the reflection but the inspiration
of Walker in the idyllic grace of Mrs. Allingham's figures and in her
treatment of flowers, place her in a company which she readily accepted and
of which she was proud.

But it was with Birket Foster that our artist's name was most intimately
linked, some commentators going to the length of asserting that without him
there would have been no Mrs. Allingham. Birket Foster himself, however,
never held that opinion, but stated that she had struck out a line which was
entirely her own, and, as he generously added, 'with much more modernity
in it than mine'.

There are, however, so many similarities between their artistic careers that
they no doubt unconsciously influenced not only the method of their work
but the subject of it.

Drawing in black and white on wood in each case formed the groundwork
of their education, and was only later followed by colour. Both, having
determined to support themselves, sought out the engravers and obtained a
livelihood from them. Birket Foster at sixteen was fortunate enough to meet
in the great wood-engraver Ebenezer Landells one who at once recognised
his capabilities, whilst, as we have seen, Mrs. Allingham found a similar

❤ ❤

AT POUND GREEN, FRESHWATER, ISLE OF WIGHT
painted 1891

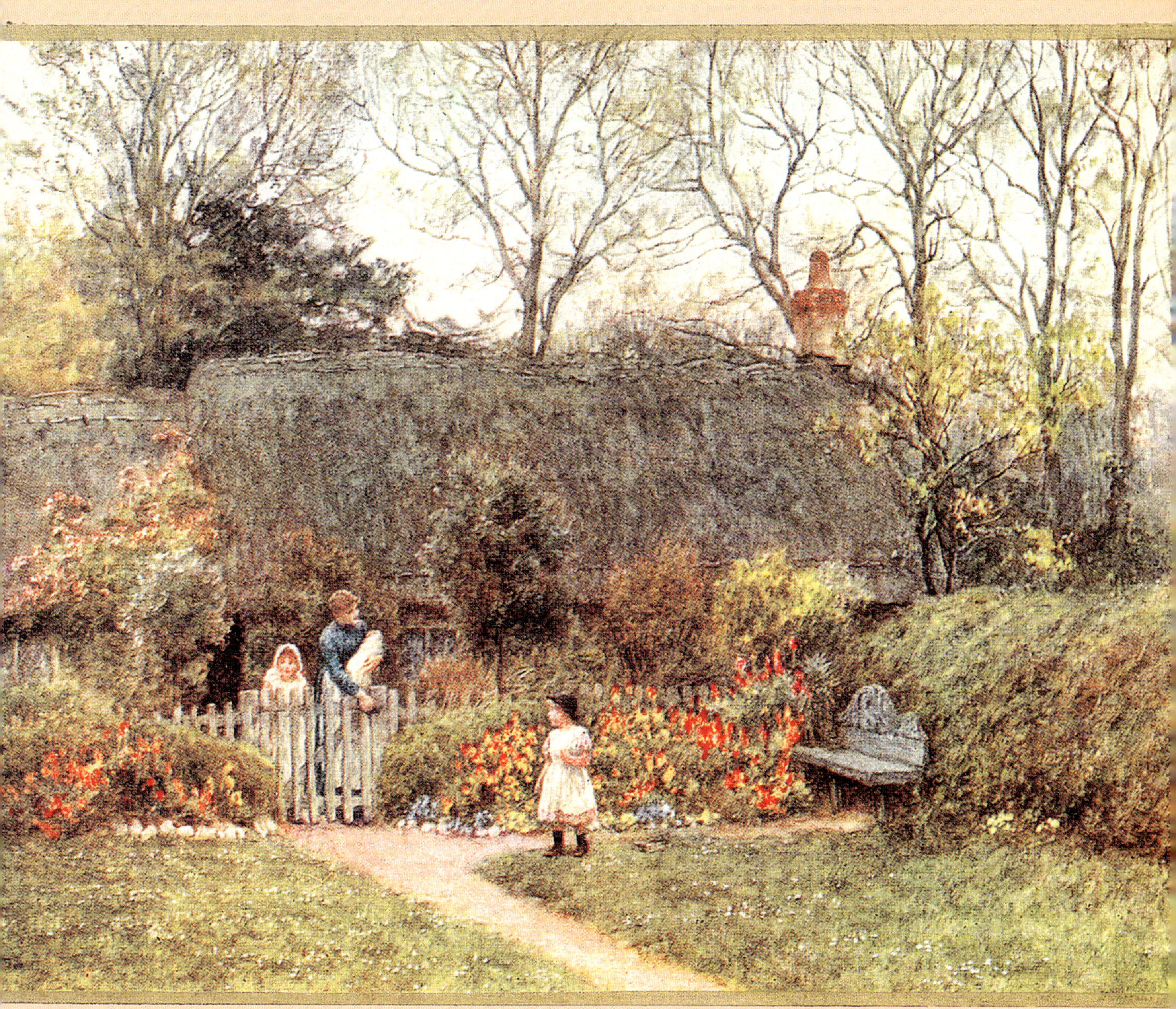

friend in Joseph Swain. Again, book illustration was as much in vogue in 1870, when our artist was embarking on her career, as it was in 1842, when Mr. Foster was in the same position. By another coincidence both years witnessed the birth of an illustrated weekly, for Birket Foster, in 1842, was employed upon the infant *Illustrated London News*, while Mrs. Allingham was the only woman to whom Mr. Thomas allotted some of the early work on the *Graphic*.

Differences there were in their opportunities, and these were not always in Mrs. Allingham's favour. Birket Foster found in Landells a man who looked after his youngster's education and, convinced that Nature was his best mistress, sent him to her with these instructions:

> Now that work is slack in these summer months, spend them in the fields; take your colours and copy every detail of the scene as carefully as possible, especially trees and foreground plants, and come up to me once a month and show me what you have done.

A splendid memory aided Foster in his studies all too well, for he learnt to draw every detail he required with such absolute fidelity that he never again needed to go to Nature. That he did so we know from his repeated visits to every part of Europe – visits resulting in delightful work; but what the world

♥♥

A Cottage at Freshwater Gate
painted 1891

Tramps were said to be rare sights on the Isle of Wight and they were even scarcer in Helen Allingham's 'perfect' world, but the figure of the woman, sending her eldest child to beg a crust of bread at the cottage door, belies it all. There is a strange twist attached to the painting of this particular cottage. The artist had nearly completed the drawing on a Saturday afternoon. A friend asked her if she would finish it the next. Whereupon she replied that she never sketched in public on Sundays. Alas, by Monday the cottage was in ruins, having burnt down the previous night.

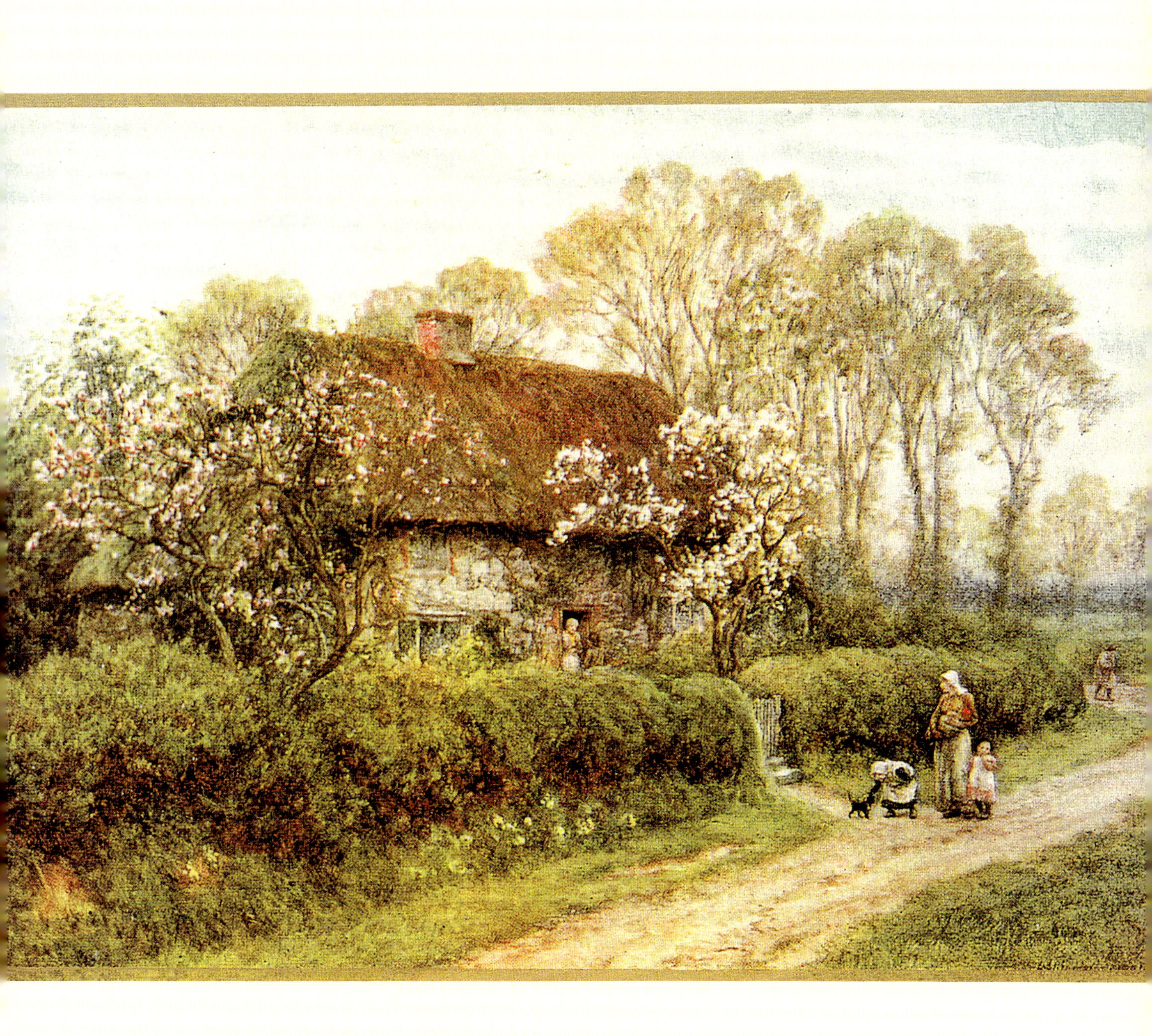

saw was entirely studio work, and this tended to a repetition which often marred the entire satisfaction that one otherwise derived from his paintings. Even Mrs. Allingham, who lived close to him and worked on the same subjects, never came across him painting out of doors and only once saw him with note-book in hand.

Chance influenced the two careers also in another way. The first commission to illustrate a book which Miss Paterson, as she then was, obtained was for a prose work, in which figures and household scenes entirely predominated – in fact, all her black-and-white work was of this homely nature – and for some years she had no call for the delineation of landscape.

With Foster it was not very different. It is true that his first commission was *The Boys' Spring and Summer Book*, in which he had to draw the seasons, and to draw them 'in the field'. But this might not have attracted him to landscape work, for his patron's next commission was quite in another direction. Certain of the young pre-Raphaelites, including Rossetti, Burne-Jones and Millais, had been entrusted with the illustration of *Evangeline*. The result completely staggered the publisher Bogue, who was absolutely incapable of appreciating their revolutionary methods.

'What shall I do with them?' he was asked by the engraver to whom he showed the blocks on which the most elaborate designs had been most lovingly drawn.

'This,' said Bogue and, wetting one of them, he erased the drawing with the sleeve of his coat, serving each in turn the same way.

❧❧

Study of a Rose Bush
painted ca 1887

This is 'Gloire de Dijon', an old favourite, begotten before the days of
scentless specimens to which are appended 'the ill-sounding names of
fashionable patrons of the rose-grower'.

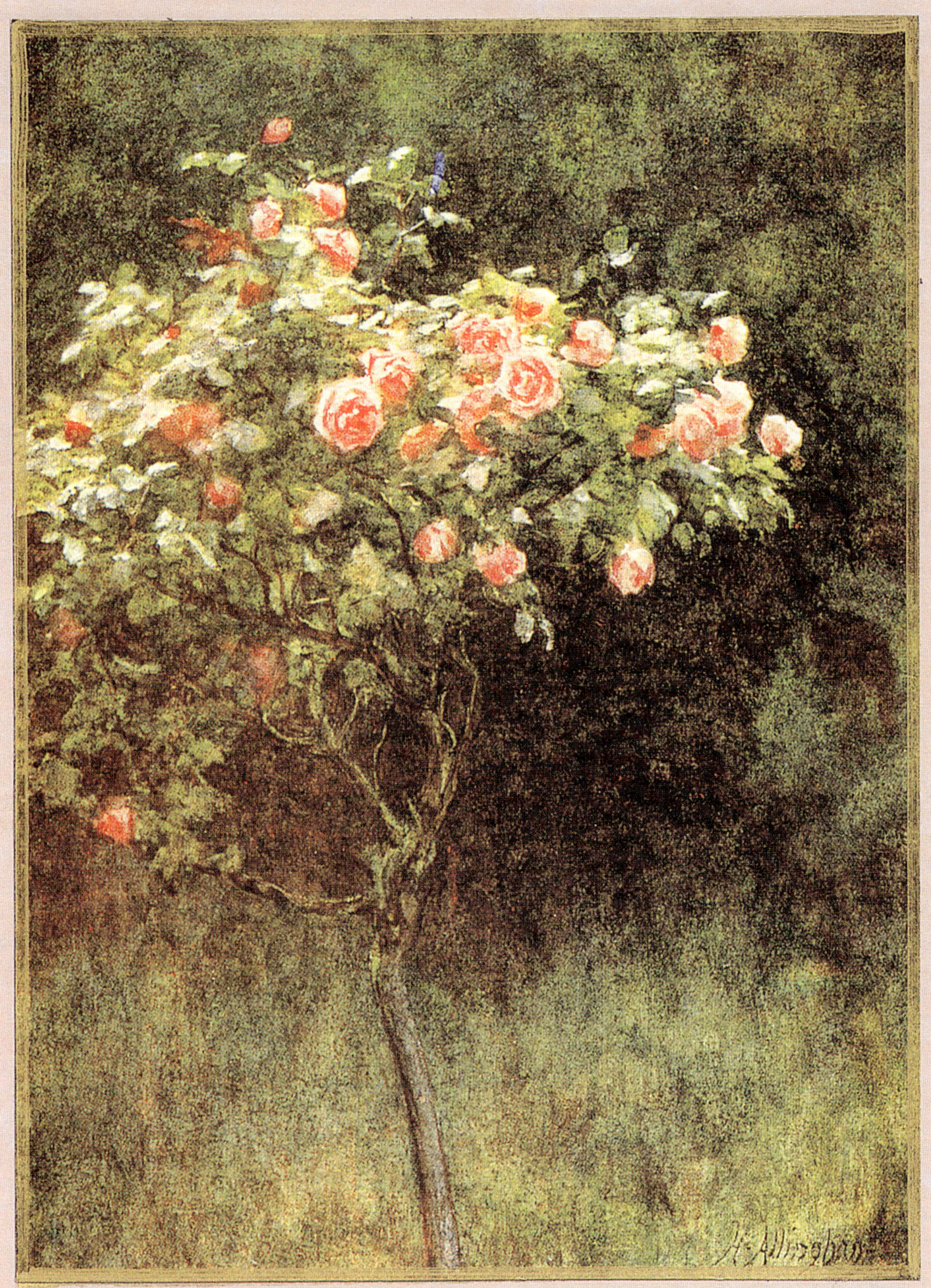

After this drastic treatment the *Evangeline* commission was handed over to Birket Foster. It can be easily imagined with what trepidation he, knowing these facts, approached and carried out his task, and what delight he felt when even the *Athenaeum* could say, 'A more lovely book than this has rarely been given to the public.' The success of the work was enormous. Birket Foster's career was apparently henceforth marked out as an illustrator of verse in black and white, for his popularity continued until it was not a question of giving him commissions, but of what book there was for him to illustrate.

Thus we see that Birket Foster's work was long confined to subjects as to which he had no voice, but which certainly influenced his art, and it says much for his temperament that throughout it warranted the term 'poetical'. Similarly it is much to Mrs. Allingham's credit that her prosaic start did not prevent the same quality welling up and being always in evidence in her productions.

Some further coincidences in their careers may also be of interest.

Birket Foster became a water-colourist through the chance that he could not sell his oil-paintings, which consequently cumbered his small working-room to such an extent that one night he cut them all from their stretchers, rolled them up and, sneaking out, dropped them over Blackfriars Bridge into the Thames; water-colours cost less to produce and took up less space, so he adopted them. Mrs. Allingham abandoned oils after a year or two's work in them at the Royal Academy Schools, because she gradually became convinced that she could express herself better in water-colours. But she considered that it was a great advantage to have worked, even for that short time, in the stronger medium. It was this practice in oils that made her for some time (until, indeed, Frederick Walker's lessons to her at the Royal Academy) use a good deal of body-colour.

❤❤

A KENTISH GARDEN
painted 1903

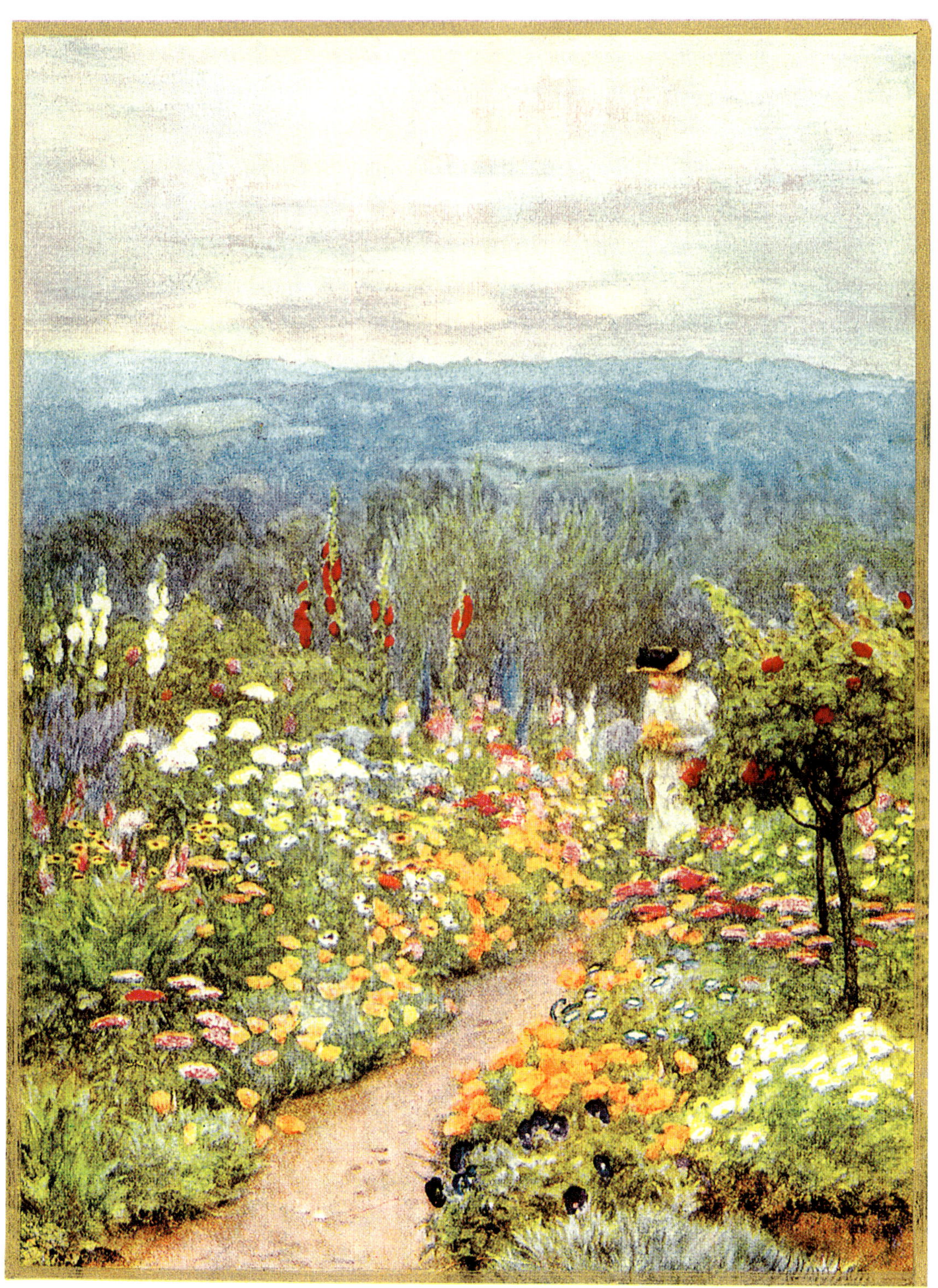

Both artists aspired to obtain the highest rank which was then open to the water-colourist, namely, membership of the Royal Water-Colour Society, but whilst Birket Foster attained it in 1860, in his thirty-fifth year and at his second attempt, Mrs. Allingham followed him in 1875, when only twenty-six and at her first essay. Both promptly gave up a remunerative income in black-and-white work and, having done so, never had cause to regret the decision.

Both, within a year or two of their election, found themselves settled near the same village, Witley, in the heart of the country which they subsequently identified with their names. Here the selection of subjects from the same neighbourhood naturally brought their work still closer together.

Lastly, few artists have been indulged with 'so many smiles and so few frowns' from the public for which they have catered. Birket Foster considered that he had been almost pampered by the critics, and Mrs. Allingham never felt she had the slightest cause to complain of her treatment at their hands.

The many resemblances between the methods of work of the two artists are no doubt due largely to the times in which they lived. Birket Foster found himself, at the start of his career, pupil of a school where composition and drawing were still thought of; before a landscape artist presumed to pose as such, he had to study the laws which governed the former, and to thoroughly imbue himself with a knowledge of the anatomy of what he was about to depict. Mrs. Allingham was also fortunate enough to commence her tuition before the fashion of undergoing this needful apprenticeship died out.

THE SOUTH BORDER
painted 1900

This was painted in Gertrude Jekyll's garden. The orange-red flowers hanging over the wall are those of the Bignonia grandiflora; *the bushes on either side of the archway with white flowers are choisyas. The adjoining flowers are red and yellow dahlias, flanked by tritonias or red-hot pokers.*

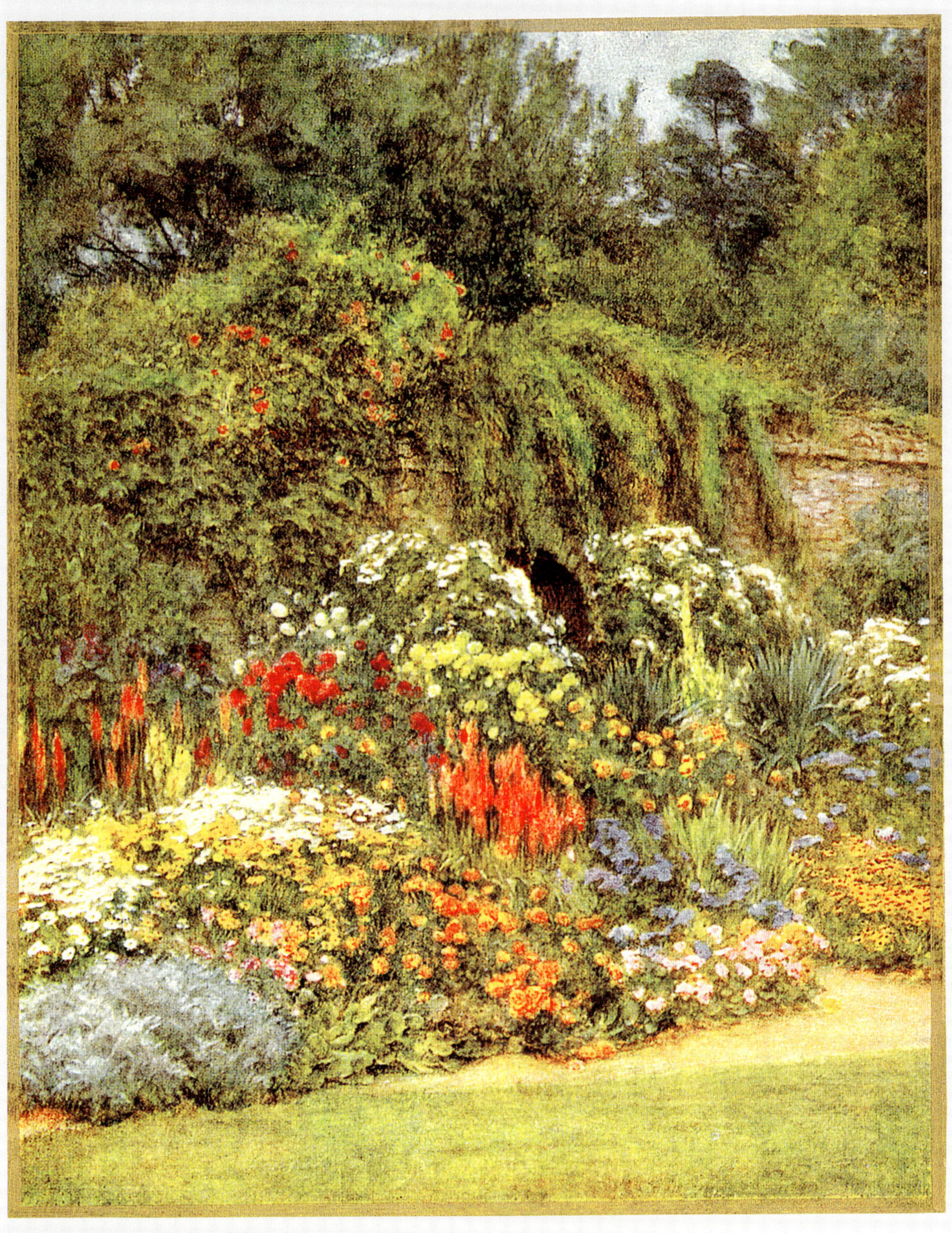

But Birket Foster came at the end of a time when landscape was painted in the studio rather than in the field. He went to Nature for suggestions, which he pencilled into note-books in the most easy and learned manner, but content with this he made his pictures under comfortable conditions at home. The fullness of his career, too, came at a time when Art was booming and the demand for his work was such that he could not keep pace with it. It is not surprising, therefore, that in the zenith of his fame his pictures were, in the main, studio pictures, worked out with a marvellous facility of invention, but nevertheless just lacking that vitality which always pervades work done in the open air and before Nature.

Mrs. Allingham's work at the outset was very similar to this. For her subject paintings she made elaborate preliminary studies from Nature in colour, but the painting itself was thought out and executed in the house. Fortunately this method soon became unpalatable to her and she gradually came to work more and more directly from Nature; when, at Witley, she found her subjects almost literally on her doorstep, she discontinued once and for ever her former method. From then on she painted every painting on the spot during the months when that was feasible, leaving completion for some time, to enable her to view her work with a fresh eye and to study at leisure such final

THE SIX BELLS
painted 1892

This beautiful old timbered ale house was discovered by Helen Allingham when staying with some artistic friends at Bearsted in Kent. Although the weather was very cold, she lost no time in painting it, as she was told that the cottage would be pulled down as soon as its owner, an old lady of ninety-two, died. Having spent a long day drawing its intricate details, the artist went into the building for a little warmth and a cup of tea. She found a farm labourer huddled over the tiny fire, with his pot of warm ale on the hob. Asking if she could sit at another fire, she was assured that none could be lit as water lay below all the floors and a fire would cause it to evaporate and fill the rooms with steam.

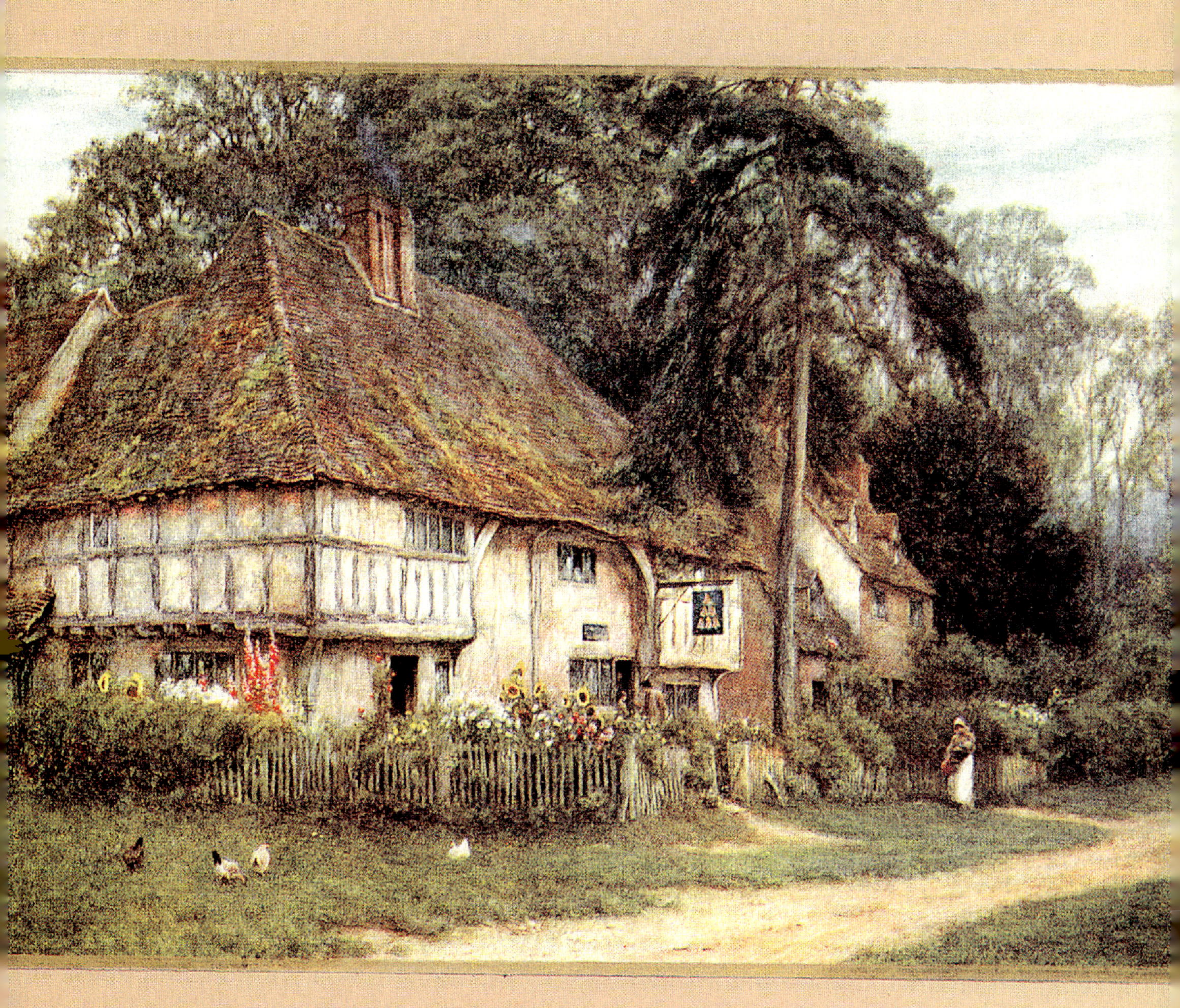

details as where the figures should be grouped. After her return to London she usually posed her models, for this purpose, in the open air in her Hampstead garden.

Her figures were, however, sometimes culled from careful studies made in note-books, of which she had an endless supply. Fastidious to a degree as to the completeness of a painting, she lingered long over the finished touches, for it was these which she considered to make or mar the whole. Every sort of contrivance she considered to be legitimate to bring about an effect, save that of body-colour, which she held in abhorrence; but the knife, a hard brush, a pointed stick, a paint rag and a sponge were always to hand.

Mrs. Allingham was above all things a fair-weather painter. She had no pleasure in the storm, whether of rain or wind. But her work was framed upon the pleasure that it afforded her, and certainly the result was no less satisfactory because it numbered only the sunny hours and the halcyon days.

The expression 'sunny hours' should perhaps be qualified, for as a rule she did not affect a sunshine which cast strong shadows, but rather its condition when, through a thin veil of cloud, it suffused all Nature with an equable light and allowed local colour to be seen at its best. In paintings which comprise any large amount of floral detail, the leaves, in full sunshine, give off an amount of reflected light that materially lessens the colour value of the flowers and prevents their being properly distinguished. George Elgood always observed this rule, not only because the effect was so much more satisfactory on paper, but because it was so much easier to paint under this aspect. As regards sky treatment, both he and Mrs. Allingham confined themselves to the simplest effects, feeling that the main interest of the painting lay on the ground, where the detail was amply sufficient to warrant the accessories being kept as subservient

❤❤

THE CUCKOO
painted 1887

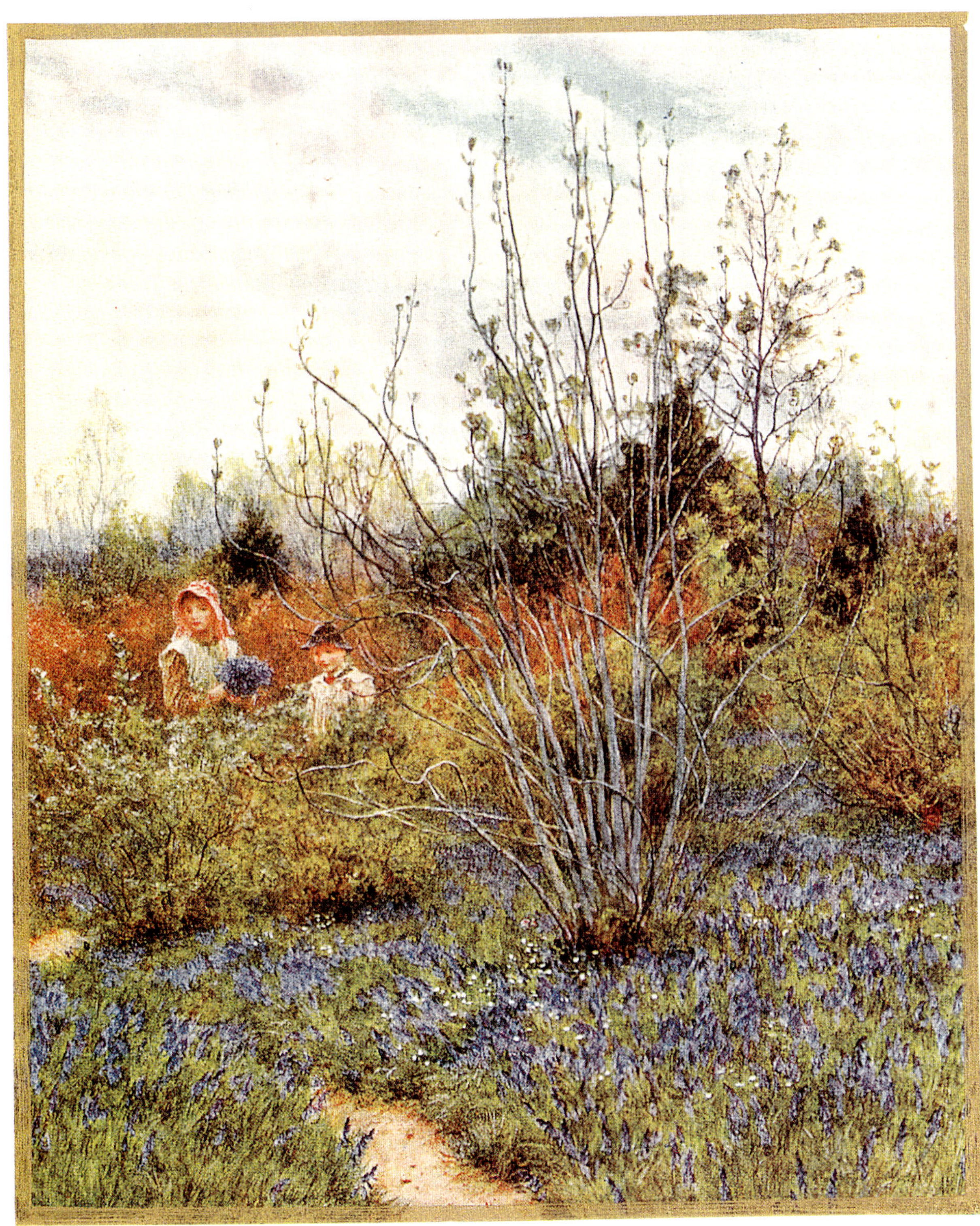

as possible. It is for this reason that the glories of sunrise and sunset have no place in Mrs. Allingham's work, the hours round midday sufficing for her needs.

To those who are curious concerning her palette, it may be said that it was of the simplest character. Her paint-box was the smallest that could hold her colours in moist cake form, of which none were used save those which she considered to be permanent. It contained cobalt, permanent yellow, aureolin, raw sienna, yellow, ochre, cadmium, rose madder, light red and sepia. She used nothing save O.W. (old water-colour) paper. Mrs. Allingham's method of laying on the colour differed from that of Birket Foster, who painted wet and in small touches. Her painting was on the dry side, letting her colours mingle on the paper. As a small bystander once remarked concerning it, 'You do mess about a deal.'

One important contemporary and friend of Mrs. Allingham's has already received a passing mention in these pages, but deserves recognition here as sharing with Mrs. Allingham the honour of being the most successful female artist of the period. Like Mrs. Allingham, Kate Greenaway was greatly admired by Ruskin, who had great influence over her choice and execution of subjects. Like Mrs. Allingham, too, she had drawn obsessively from childhood; as a student of the Royal College she won a Bronze Medal for her decorative art when she was but fifteen and went on to study at the Slade School, where in the early 1870s she first met the young Helen Paterson. In her twenties she executed commissions for *The People's Magazine* and *The Illustrated London News,* as well as illustrating children's novels and greeting cards in the charming style which made her a household name. Mrs. Allingham was already an admirer of her work before the two women became friends: she is quoted as saying that 'no one could draw roses like Kate Greenaway'.

❤❤

HEATHER ON CROCKHAM HILL, KENT
painted 1902

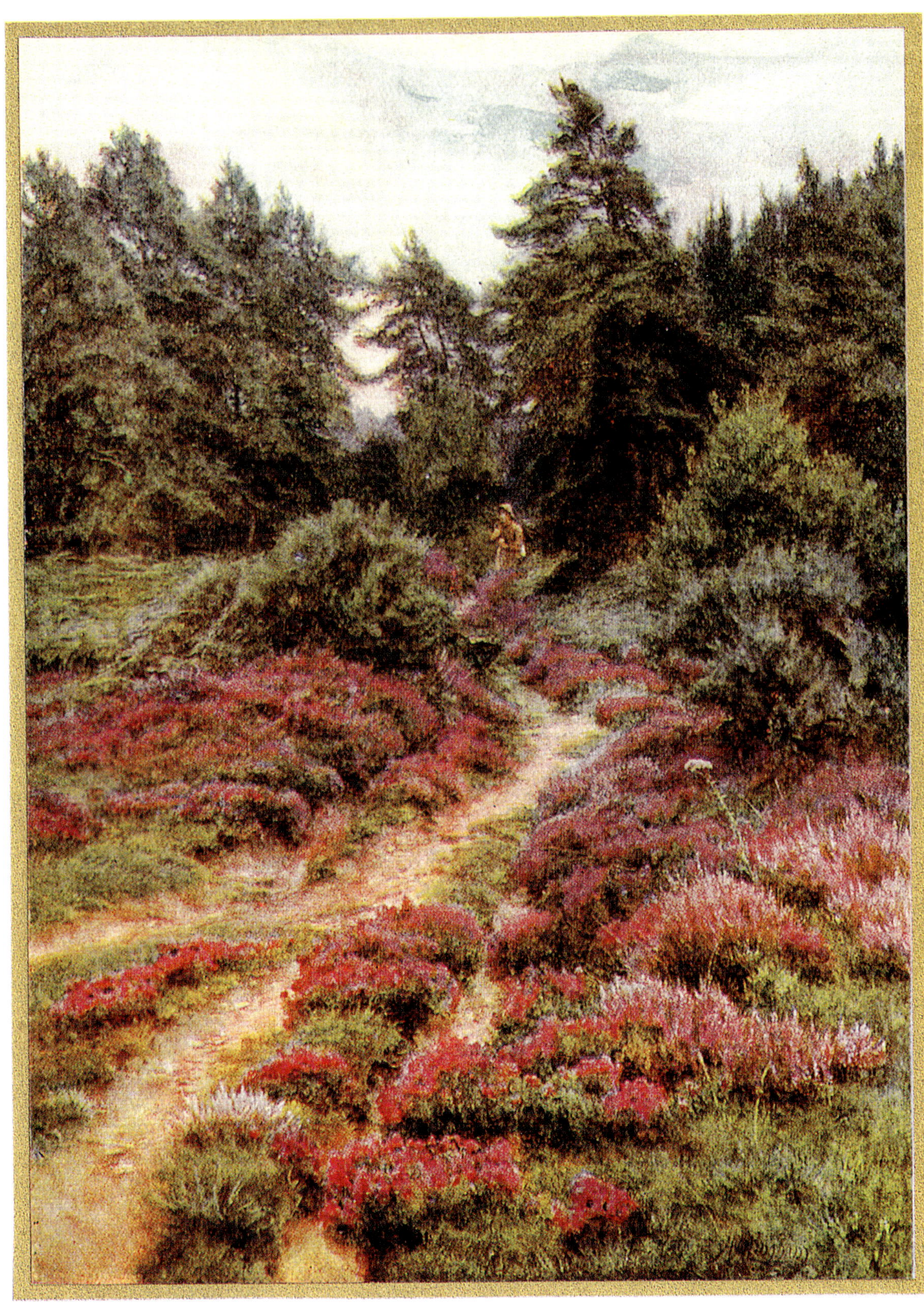

Miss Greenaway was fortunate in being able to work with Edmund Evans, the pioneer colour engraver, whose techniques enabled her work to be reproduced with purer and more realistic colour and tone than had hitherto been possible. It was through Evans, another resident of Witley, with whom she often went to stay, that she became friendly with the Allinghams. Although they met a number of times over a period of years, Mrs. Allingham remembered that it was only in the spring of 1888, when they went out painting together in the copses near Witley that they became really *friends*. Writing after Miss Greenaway's death in 1901, she recalled the intimacy of the following years:

> One day in the autumn of 1889 we went to Pinner together on an exploring expedition for subjects, and were delighted with some of the old cottages we saw there. I had been pressing her ever since our spring time together at Witley to share with me some of the joys of painting out of doors. Another day we went further afield – the Chesham and Amersham. She was delighted with the beauty of the country and the picturesque old towns.

> I am afraid that her short sight must have greatly added to the difficulty of out-door painting for her. I remember her exclaiming one day at Pinner, 'What am I to do? When I look at the roof it is all a red blur – when I put on my spectacles I see every crack in the tiles.'

❤❤

ON IDE HILL
painted 1900

Ide Hill is to be found in Kent, on the south side of the Westerham Valley, and this cottage was one of the last survivors of this type of dwellings in the area, every one having been replaced by 'the newly built and commonplace'. It is possible that the local inhabitants did not so much lament their disappearance. The local doctor, upon seeing another woman painter, Octavia Hill, sketching the same view, asked her why she had selected a house that had had more fever in it than any other in the entire parish!

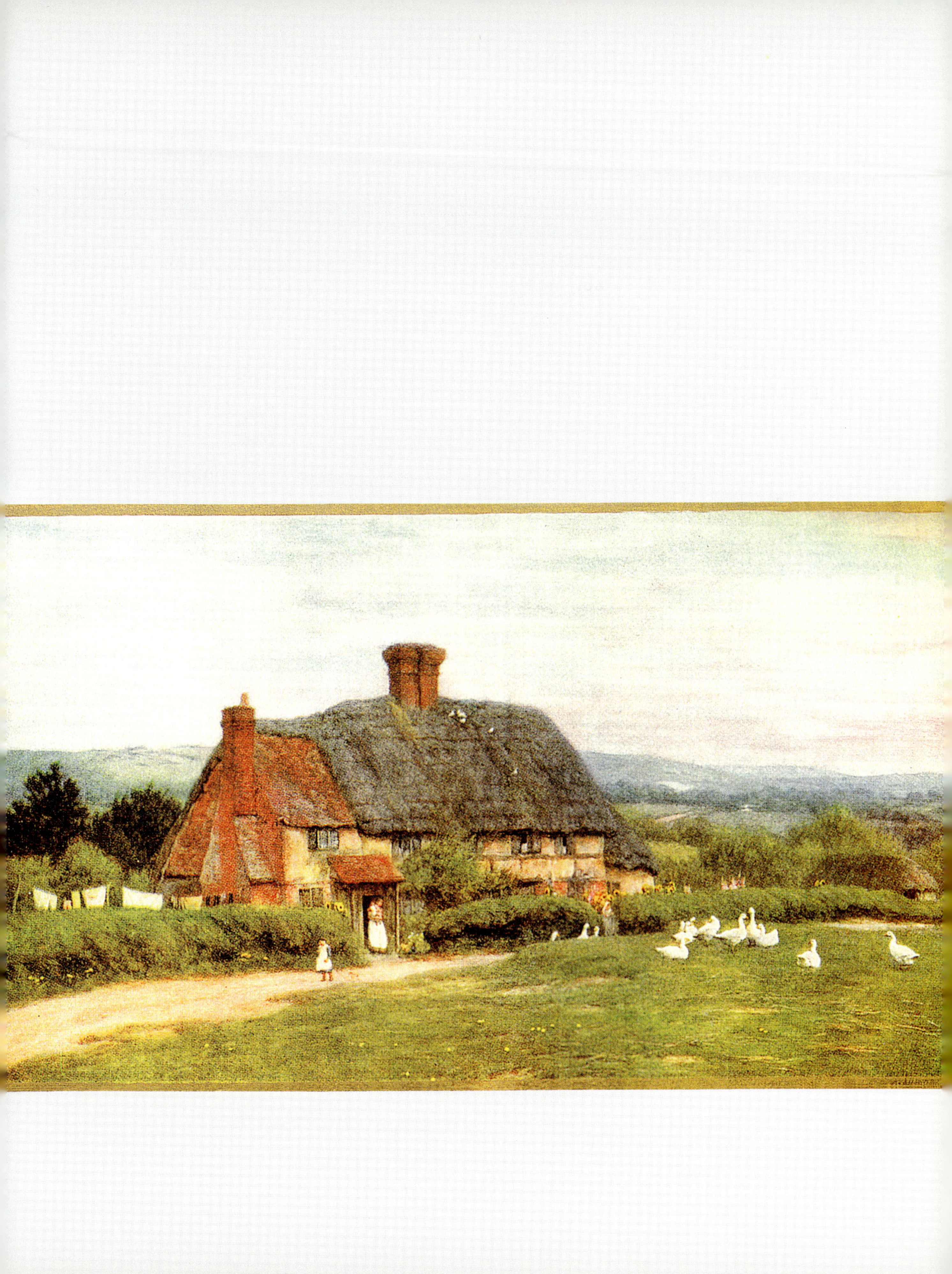

Though we often sat side by side, painting the same object (generally silently, for she was a very earnest, hard worker – and perhaps I was, too), it seemed to me that there was little likeness between our drawings – especially after the completion in the studio. But she was one of the most sensitive of creatures and I think she felt that it might be wiser for us both to discontinue the practice of working from the same subjects, so, after that summer of 1890, we did not go out painting any more together. Whether days or months passed between our meetings, I was always sure of the same hearty greeting from her.

It remains to mention two contemporaries of Mrs. Allingham's with whom her work has been compared; and one younger neighbour on whom she may be said to have had an influence.

Wilmot Pilsbury had also studied in Birmingham and come to London to qualify as an art teacher. In 1870 he returned to the Midlands as head of the Leicester School of Art, and his work from that time on reflects his intimate knowledge of the nearby farms and meadows. Like Mrs. Allingham he was meticulous in his representation of local detail: just as her cottages bear the identifying features of Kent and Sussex discussed earlier, so the buildings and features of his work site it clearly in Leicestershire.

John Fulleylove was also from Leicester and began his career with a firm of architects. A continuing interest in architecture pervades much of his work: the rustic cottages of his paintings are more boldly delineated and less idyllically treated than those of Mrs. Allingham.

Walter Tyndale settled in Haslemere in about 1890, having studied in Belgium, where he was born, and begun his career painting portraits and working largely in oils. Fifteen years younger than Mrs. Allingham, he may have been influenced by her work, or simply inspired by the same countryside that had inspired so much of her early work.

A few words will suffice to summarise the latter part of Mrs. Allingham's career. In the autumn of 1888 she and her husband left Witley and returned to live in London. Thereafter she remained at the same address in Hampstead for the rest of her long life. William Allingham died in 1889, after which his widow devoted some time to editing his diaries, which were published in 1907.

As an artist she was at her most successful during the 1890s. With the start of the new century she made various efforts to broaden her range of subjects, travelling to Venice and producing a few paintings based on her experiences there, but the ensuing exhibition was one of the least successful of her career. Indeed, although she continued to paint and to exhibit with the Institute of Painters in Water Colours until the year of her death (1926), it is fair to say that by 1903, the date of the latest paintings included in this volume, she had completed her finest work.

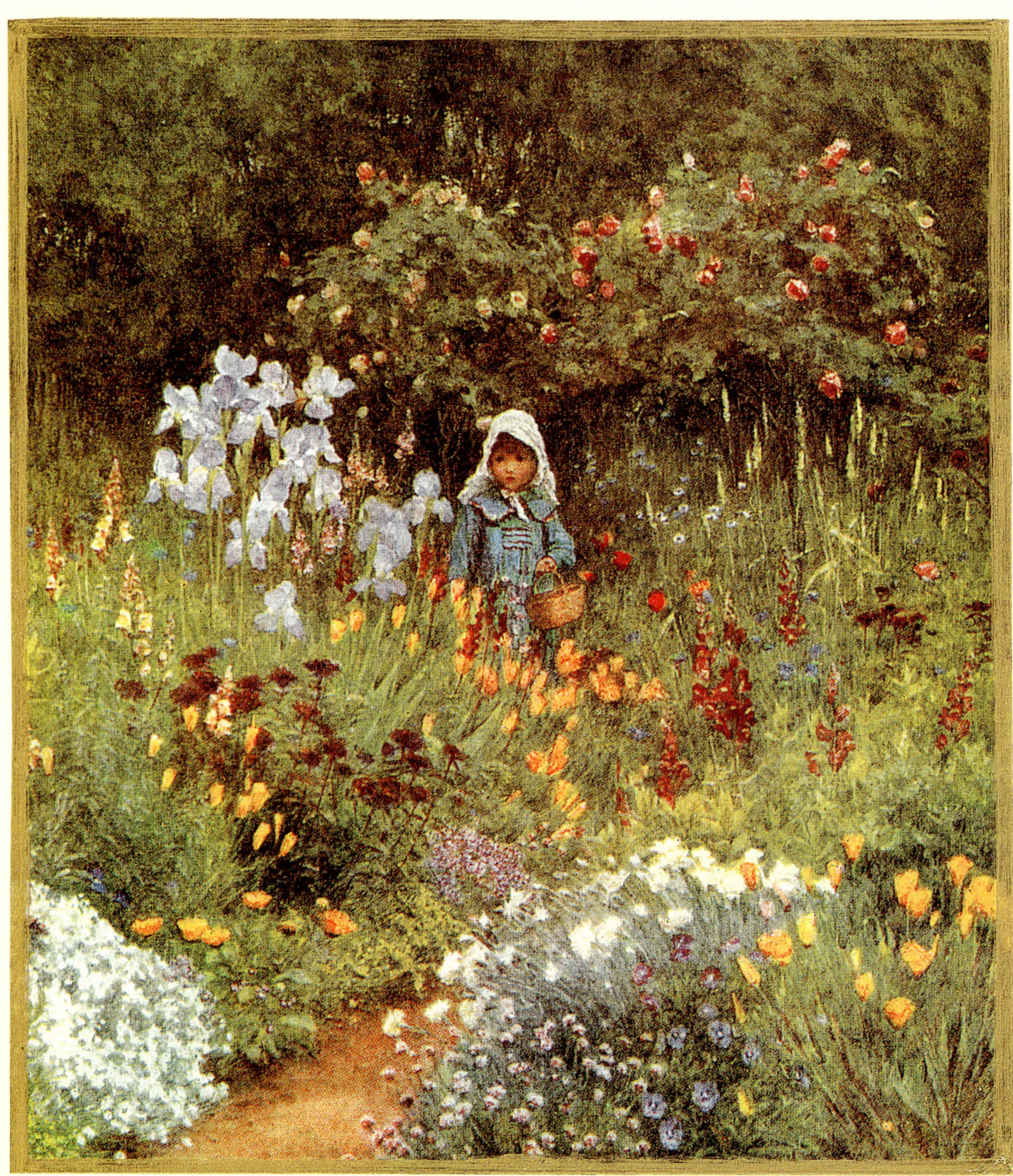